ĀṆṬĀḶ

And Her Path of Love

Sri Garib Dass Oriental Series No. 137

ĀṆṬĀḶ
And Her Path of Love

Poems of a Woman Saint From South India

Vidya Dehejia

Sri Satguru Publications
A Division of
Indian Books Centre
Delhi-India

Published by :
SRI SATGURU PUBLICATIONS
Indological and Oriental Publishers
A Division of
Indian Books Centre
40/5, Shakti Nagar,
Delhi-110007
(INDIA)

First Indian Edition : Delhi, 1992

ISBN 81-7030-313-3

Cover Photograph : Bronze image of Āṇṭāḷ Śrīvilliputtūr temple, Ca. 970. The worn condition of the bronze is the result of centuries of ritual worship. Courtesy of the Dr. R. Nagaswamy

Printed in India

Contents

Acknowledgments

In presenting to the reader this volume of the poems of Āṇṭāḷ, woman saint and mystic of the ninth century, I have seen my role primarily as translator. I have attempted to stay close to both the words and spirit of the original poems, steering a middle path between a literal and a free translation. Such interpretative comment as is inevitable in a translation of this nature has been confined largely to the introduction and notes. While it is hoped that the introductory essay will enable the reader to recapture Āṇṭāḷ's very special appropriation of the world of Hindu Vaiṣṇava myth, it does not claim to provide a sustained study of Āṇṭāḷ's mysticism.

Transliteration has posed a problem, since the poems of Tamil *bhakti*, while composed in a Dravidian language, nevertheless draw upon a Sanskrit vocabulary. In both the translation and the commentary, Tamil words are transliterated according to the system employed in the Madras University Tamil Lexicon, while Sanskrit words are transliterated according to the standard system. However, several Sanskrit loan words are not immediately apparent in their Tamil versions; these are transliterated variously, in either Sanskrit or Tamil, depending on whether they overtly display their source of origin or appear to have been integrated into Tamil.

I owe a debt of gratitude to my Tamil pundit, Vidwan M. Viswanathan of the Bangalore Tamil Sangam, who guided me through Āṇṭāḷ's poetry and the Maṇipravāḷa prose of later commentators and hagiographers. I am much indebted to my colleagues, both in India and the United States, in particular to K.K.A. Venkatachari, Dennis Hudson, Norman Cutler and H. Daniel Smith, who afforded me enlightening glimpses into Tamil Vaiṣṇava *bhakti*. In a special category is A.K. Ramanujan who some ten years back first encouraged me, an art historian, to enter the realm of Tamil poetry. Finally, I would like to express my appreciation to my mother, Sankari Rama Iyer, who accompanied me along the path in search of Āṇṭāḷ, and whose perceptive observations deepened my understanding of bhakti poetry; to her I dedicate this book.

Introduction: Woman, Poet, and Mystic

Āṇṭāḷ and the Saints of South India

In the Tamil country of South India, between the sixth and the tenth centuries, there emerged a remarkable group of holy men and women who transformed the religious milieu of the south. Blazing a trail for the path of love, they emphasized utter surrender to a personal god whom they approached on intimate terms, as child, friend, slave or lover. They composed poems in praise of their deity, frequently using as their model the poems that glorified their monarch, and at times adapting popular ballads to their use. Most of these hymns (poems) were set to music, in many instances to melodies prevalent among the people, thus making their verses accessible to the masses. So strong was the influence of these saints that South India, once dominated by the faiths of Jainism and Buddhism, now became a stronghold of Hindu worship.

These holy persons were referred to as Nāyaṉmārs or leaders if they were devotees of god Śiva, and as Āḻvārs or "those who dive deep (into the divine)" if they worshipped Viṣṇu. There were sixty–three Nāyaṉmārs of Śiva, of whom several appear to have been legendary figures, and twelve Āḻvārs of Viṣṇu, all of whom were historical personages who composed poetry. Āṇṭāḷ, known also as Kōtai or "She of the fragrant tresses," was one of the twelve Āḻvārs of Viṣṇu,[1] and the only woman amongst them.

The saints of South India acquired a position of such great eminence that a cult arose around them. Bronze images of both Nāyaṉmārs and Āḻvārs were commissioned by every temple for placement in the innermost courtyard beside the sanctum sanctorum. Frequently temples commissioned a second set of images, usually of stone, while quite often their portraits were painted on the temple walls. Their images were bathed, clothed, and adorned, and ritual worship was offered to them in a manner similar to that accorded to the deity of the temple. There were special observances in the temples on their birthdays and death anniversaries, and these ceremonies included a recital of their hymns. The twelve Āḻvārs were given a unique status since they were considered to be *amśas* or secondary incarnations of Viṣṇu's companions and his attributes. Pride of position in this scheme went to Kōtai who was regarded as an *amśa* of Viṣṇu's second consort Bhūdevī, the goddess earth. The title Āṇṭāḷ as "she who rules (the lord)" was assigned to her because she achieved the closest possible relationship with Lord Viṣṇu.

Āṇṭāḷ's Place among the Āḻvārs

The twelve Vaiṣṇava saints span a period of three centuries from roughly 600–900 A.D. The earliest among them are a group of three saints known as the Mutal, or First Āḻvārs who may be placed in the early seventh century, while the latest is that most revered saint Nammāḻvār and his disciple Maturakavi who belong around the year 900 A.D. It would appear that the woman saint Āṇṭāḷ lived soon after the year 800 A.D. The evidence for this date is indirect and depends largely upon the date assigned to saint Periyāḻvār or Viṣṇucitta, her father by adoption. In one of his poems, Periyāḻvār refers to a ruling Pāṇṭiya monarch Neṭumāṟan as one who extolled the lord of Tirumāliruñcōlai (Viṣṇu). By and large, the Pāṇṭiya rulers were staunch Śaivites, and the only monarch referred to in the inscriptions as a *parama vaiṣṇava* or great Vaiṣṇava is Jaṭila Parāntaka, who ruled from 765–815 A.D., and was also known as Neṭun–jataiyaṉ and Māṟan–jaṭaiyaṉ. However, it is also possible that Periyāḻvār was referring to the next Pāṇṭiya ruler, Śrīmāra Śrīvallabha, who though not specifically hailed as a Vaiṣṇava, was known as Neṭumāṟaṉ and was monarch from 815–862 A.D.[2] Periyāḻvār and Āṇṭāḷ would appear to have been prominent in the first half of the ninth century.

Several attempts have been made to date Āṇṭāḷ on the basis of astronomical observations contained in her *Tiruppāvai*. Her assertion, in its first song, that it is the full moon day of the month of Mārkaḷi, when combined with her statement in song thirteen that "Venus has risen/Jupiter has gone to slumber," has led scholars to propose the date of November 27, 850 for the composition of the poem. However, as Filliozat points out in his detailed discussion of astronomical dating,[3] it is possible to find such a concomitance of planets in several other centuries, and a date of 731 A.D., for example, is equally feasible. According to an alternate system of calculation, based on astronomical data contained in the fourteenth century hagiographical text, the *Kuruparamparāpirapāvam 6000*, certain scholars have suggested a date of May 27, 725 (or May 29, 1205) for the birth of Āṇṭāḷ. A thirteenth century date may certainly be ruled out, and while the correspondence of dates in the eighth century is intriguing, it would appear that the most persuasive date for Āṇṭāḷ is the year 850, suggested both by song thirteen of *Tiruppāvai*, and the historical data regarding Pāṇṭiya king Neṭumāraṉ.

The Āḻvārs were part of a *bhakti* movement in the Tamil country which resulted in the overthrow of the Jain and Buddhist faiths and the establishment of the supremacy of Hindu worship. The prime movers in this movement appear to have been the Śaiva saints, in particular the two seventh century Nāyaṉmārs, Campantar and Appar, who actively confronted the heterodox faiths, defying their leaders and challenging their authority, proposing debates and performing miracles. According to hagiographic accounts, Campantar conclusively defeated the Jains, largely by the display of miraculous power, and converted the Pāṇṭiya monarch of Maturai to the worship of Śiva; Appar, by similar means, won over the Pallava ruler of Kāñcipuram. Campantar, in particular, expressed himself strongly and vociferously against these heterodox sects. He composed over four hundred *patikams*, songs consisting of ten or eleven verses, and he generally allocated the tenth verse of each *patikam* to the condemnation of the Buddhists and Jains. Other Śaiva saints, including eighth century Cuntarar and ninth century Māṇikkavācakar continued this stance of hostility and opposition, although perhaps to a lesser degree. The Āḻvārs, by and large, did not enter the fray or participate in dispute and argument. While they appear to have approved of the resistance offered by the Śaiva saints, they contented themselves with occasional disparagement of the Buddhists and Jains. Vaiṣṇava hagiography narrates only one instance of confrontation in its tale of Tirumaṅkai Āḻvār removing a golden image of the Buddha from a monastery at Nākapaṭṭinam, melting it down and using the gold to cover the temple spire at Śrīraṅkam. In general, the Āḻvārs appear to have preferred quietly to propagate the path of Viṣṇu bhakti and sing the praises of their lord. Their devotional fervor and incessant adoration of Viṣṇu is reflected in the four thousand devotional verses that they composed.

Most of the Āḻvārs divided their devotion between the various forms of Viṣṇu. For instance, monarch–saint Kulasēkhara sang of the primal form of Viṣṇu as lord of Araṅkam, lord of Vēṅkaṭa, lord of Vittuvakoṭu; he sang of infant Rāma, and Rāma in banishment; he sang also of baby Kṛṣṇa. However both Periyāḻvār and Āṇṭāḷ sang almost exclusively of Kṛṣṇa. Periyāḻvār composed a single hymn devoted to the primal form of Viṣṇu, while his *Periya Tirumoḻi*, a corpus of fifty songs, praises Kṛṣṇa.

Āṇṭāḷ wrote two works, both dedicated to Kṛṣṇa—the popular *Tiruppāvai* of thirty verses and the relatively unknown and neglected *Nācciyār Tirumoḻi*, a set of fourteen hymns in one hundred and forty–three verses. Today, the *Tiruppāvai* is sung especially by young unmarried girls during the month of Mārkaḻi (December–January). Its popularity may be attributed to the belief that taking a vow to bathe at dawn each day of the month and to sing Āṇṭāḷ's thirty verses will bring maidens an early and happy marriage. Recorded versions of the *Tiruppāvai* are readily available, and its verses may be heard throughout the month of Mārkaḻi over the official Indian radio network of South India. There are at least four translations of its verses into English, and one into French.[4] By contrast the *Nācciyār Tirumoḻi* is lesser known and is not chanted in temples or at religious festivals, and only a single English translation of its hymns exists.[5] Its mode may be classified as bridal mysticism and Āṇṭāḷ uses the lover–beloved mode, one of the accepted ways of approach to the godhead. Āṇṭāḷ's uninhibited expression of the pain of separation from the beloved and her incessant yearning for his presence, added to an occasional use of sexual terminology, appears to have been responsible, in part, for its neglect. Most devotees would find it difficult to relate to this mode. In fact, it was only after three years of studying the hymns of the saints that I was finally able to persuade my Tamil pundit that we should take up the study of the *Nācciyār Tirumoḻi* or "Sacred Song of the Lady." Only the sixth song of this work, the marriage hymn commencing with the words "*Vāranamāyiram*," is widely known; it is, in fact, recited at many Vaiṣṇava weddings in South India. Brides regard Āṇṭāḷ with special reverence and frequently young Vaiṣṇava girls are bedecked as Āṇṭāḷ on their wedding day in the hope that divine favor may descend upon them.

Another reason for the exclusion of the *Nācciyār Tirumoḻi* from temple rituals lies in the fact, aptly pointed out by Dennis Hudson, that its hymns are the expression of a singular, individual path to god, a "solitary unitive experience,"[6] that is quite inapplicable as a mode of worship for the general populace. Clearly, it is the communal ideal of the *Tiruppāvai* that has led to its position of supreme importance in temple ritual, and to the corresponding neglect of the *Nācciyār Tirumoḻi* which describes the unique path of a single saint.

Śrīvilliputtūr and the Legend of Āṇṭāḷ

In the temple of Śrīvilliputtūr in Tamilnāṭu, the first puja of the day, performed at dawn, includes an extraordinary rite which infringes all *śāstric* tradition. This rite, faithfully observed each morning, involves the transference of Āṇṭāḷ's discarded garland of the evening before to the person of the majestic reclining Viṣṇu. Hindu ritual ordains that flowers offered to the godhead must be absolutely pure; used flowers, those which have dropped to the ground, those which have been smelled or otherwise "polluted," are taboo. In fact, hagiographic tradition narrates the story of a Śaiva saint who cut off a queen's nose for having smelled a flower set aside for the worship of Śiva; it further informs us that the king, equally perturbed by this act of pollution, cut off the hand that picked up the flower with the intention of smelling it.[7] In such a context, the singular nature of the rite of the discarded garland at the temple of Śrīvilliputtūr becomes doubly significant.

As the temple doors open at dawn, preparations are afoot for the *uṣā–kāla* (dawn) puja which is first performed in the Āṇṭāḷ shrine. At the completion of this worship, even as the richly garbed bronze image of Āṇṭāḷ stands freshly garlanded, the partially wilted garland which she had worn all night is carried in procession through the temple to the shrine of the reclining Raṅkanāta. At the appropriate moment in the morning puja of Viṣṇu, Āṇṭāḷ's discarded garland is placed ceremonially around his neck. At noon, this same garland travels to the shrine of Āṇṭāḷ's father Periyāḻvār, and is offered to him. Honored visitors to the temple of Śrīvilliputtūr may be blessed by having Āṇṭāḷ's discarded garland placed momentarily upon them, and they may be given one of its wilted flowers as *prasātam.* This unique ritual, in which the wilted garland worn by Āṇṭāḷ the previous evening is placed upon the image of the mighty Lord Viṣṇu, is a daily reenactment of a crucial point in the legendary story of Āṇṭāḷ's bhakti, her total rejection of human love, her longing for union with the lord, and the lord's ultimate acceptance of her as a special devotee and as his bride.

Śrīvilliputtūr is today a modest town with a population of 150,000. Little remains to remind us of its erstwhile prosperity or its magnificent "storeyed mansions" so proudly described by Āṇṭāḷ in the signature verses of the fourteen poems that comprise her *Nācciyār Tirumoḻi.* Only the famous temple with its single towering *gopuram,* the tallest in all of Tamilnāṭu, stands witness, both outwardly and in its ritual worship, to Āṇṭāḷ's bhakti and her fame as a saint. One may note that the *gopuram* is in direct alignment with the shrine of the reclining Raṅkanāta which was the original focus of the temple. The Āṇṭāḷ shrine, which contains a standing image of Viṣṇu as Raṅkamannār with Āṇṭāḷ as his consort to the left and Garuḍa to the right, is located off–center within the temple complex and is clearly a later addition.

The *Śrīvilliputtūr Sthala Purāṇa*[8] confirms that the shrine of reclining Viṣṇu is the original sanctum of the temple. This mythical account of the temple, which draws on hagiographic texts, but is written in a popular and naive style, explains the name of the town as being the new town (*puttūr*) built by a chieftain named Villi; the word Śrī was added because the goddess Lakṣmī, as Āṇṭāḷ, chose to take up her abode there.[9] The hunter–chieftain Villi, following the instructions received from Viṣṇu in a dream, searched for an image of reclining Viṣṇu, and having found one in a forest, he built a shrine to enclose the image, and later constructed a town around the temple. The *Sthala Purāṇa* further relates that Viṣṇu's consort Bhūdevī (goddess earth) asked as a boon of Viṣṇu that she be born on earth as his greatest devotee. In the spiritual context it is believed that on earth alone, and in a human body alone, can one experience the bliss of longing for the divine and feel the divine presence. The *Purāṇa* relates that Viṣṇu responded to Bhūdevī's request and blessed her to be daughter to Periyāḻvār. It was thus that one day Viṣṇucitta, a priest at the Śrīvilliputtūr temple, discovered an infant girl lying amidst the *tulasī* bushes (sacred basil) surrounding his home.

Hagiographic Accounts of the Life of Āṇṭāḷ

Two main documents, both hagiographies, constitute our prime source of information for the legend of Āṇṭāḷ. The first is the fourteenth–century text, *Kuruparamparāpirapāvam 6000* or "6000 Verses on the Glory of the Succession of the Gurus," composed by Piṉpaḻakiya Perumāḷ Jīyar[10] in mixed Sanskrit and Tamil known as Maṇipravāḷa (*maṇi* = crystal:Sanskrit; *pravāḷa* = coral:Tamil). The second is the Sanskrit poem *Divyasūricaritam* or "Characters of the Sacred Ones" by Garuḍavāhana Paṇḍita, assigned at one time to the twelfth century, but in recent scholarship reassigned to the fifteenth century.

The Tamil hagiography commences the life of Āṇṭāḷ by comparing Śrīvilliputtūr with the sacrificial ground where Sītā was found by Janaka, and informs us that Bhūdevī manifested herself as an infant girl at the spot where Viṣṇucitta was hoeing the ground for his sacred basil. Naming the child Kōtai of the fragrant tresses, Viṣṇucitta raised her as if she were the goddess Śrī. As a very young girl, she would, in her father's absence, adorn herself in bridal garb and wrap around her glossy tresses the long garland that had been prepared and set aside for the evening puja of Viṣṇu. Thus adorned, she would gaze into a mirror to see if she looked a bride fit for the lord. She would then return the garland to its place, and Viṣṇucitta, unaware of the "desecration," would offer the garland to Viṣṇu. Many days passed in this manner until the Āḻvār discovered Kōtai's secret. Deeply perturbed by the flagrant disregard of *śāstric* rules, Viṣṇucitta performed the evening puja without making an offering of the garland. That night, Viṣṇu appeared to him in a dream and told him that the garland worn by Āṇṭāḷ was especially dear to him and had an added fragrance. Viṣṇucitta realized that Āṇṭāḷ was no ordinary child but had in her a touch of the divine. Wondering if Piṉṉai, Nīlādevī or Śrīdevī had taken birth thus, he gave his daughter the name of *cūṭi–koṭutta–nācciyār*, meaning "lady who gave what she had worn."

Now more than ever, Āṇṭāḷ set her heart on the lord and totally rejected the idea of marriage with a mere mortal; she would be the bride of none but Viṣṇu. Āṇṭāḷ's days were passed increasingly in the contemplation of Viṣṇu and it was at this time, according to the hagiography, that she composed her *Tiruppāvai* and *Nācciyār Tirumoḻi*. Āṇṭāḷ was firm in saying she would look at none other than Viṣṇu. Since the lord had manifested himself in one hundred and eight sacred places, Viṣṇucitta wondered which of these forms she had in mind. In response to Āṇṭāḷ's request, he sang in praise of the character and deeds of each of the many forms, and as Āṇṭāḷ listened to the beauty of the lord of Śrīraṅkam, she was overcome by the intensity of a love which arose from the depths of her being.

Āṇṭāḷ's single–minded absorption with the lord of Śrīraṅkam filled Viṣṇucitta with deep anxiety for his daughter. But the lord appeared to him in a dream and assured him that he, Viṣṇu, would accept Āṇṭāḷ as his bride. It is said that Viṣṇu himself arranged for Kōtai to be brought from Śrīvilliputtūr in full bridal regalia, accompanied by all the fanfare of a royal marriage party. When the bridal procession arrived at the sanctum of reclining Raṅkanāta at Śrīraṅkaṃ, Āṇṭāḷ emerged from the curtained palanquin, walked up to the image, embraced the feet of the lord, and climbed upon the serpent couch only to vanish mysteriously. She had merged with the beautiful temple Raṅkanāta, stone symbol of her beloved! The lord addressed Viṣṇucitta as his father–in–law, offered him honors, and requested him to return to Śrīvilliputtūr and continue to serve him in that temple.

The Sanskrit poem, *Divyasūricaritam*, varies from the Maṇipravāḷa account only in minor details; however, it elaborates upon the story towards its conclusion, informing us, for instance, that Viṣṇucitta took his daughter to Nammālvār to obtain his blessings for the marriage. The poem also adds to the importance of Śrīvilliputtūr by relating that after the miraculous merger at Śrīraṅkam, a formal marriage was celebrated in Āṇṭāḷ's home town on the full moon day of the month of Paṅkuṉi. The author devotes almost four chapters of his poem to a description of this glorious wedding which was attended by all the Āḻvārs.

Āṇṭāḷ, from Her Own Poetry

The only historical material that we possess regarding the life of Āṇṭāḷ is the internal evidence of her poems. The *Tiruppāvai* and each of the fourteen hymns of the *Nācciyār Tirumoḻi* ends with a signature verse in which Āṇṭāḷ indicates her relationship with Periyāḻvār, using the words "Kōtai of Viṣṇucittaṉ," (Periyāḻvār), or "Kōtai of the chief of brahmins" (*paṭṭar-pirāṉkōtai*); presumably she was his adopted daughter, although she does not specify this. It is intriguing to note that in five signature verses she refers to Viṣṇucitta as *kōṉ* (king) of Villiputtūr or Putuvai, while three verses variously describe him as *maṉ*, *maṉṉaṉ*, and *nampi* (all meaning lord, chief or master). Unless we choose to explain such words as serving a purely rhetorical function, the implication seems to be that in addition to being a *paṭṭar* priest who served at the temple of Villiputtūr, Viṣṇucitta had an additional status akin to that of chieftain, perhaps mayor. Kōtai also hints at her own beauty, describing herself in the signature verses of the *Nācciyār Tirumoḻi* as "she of the long tresses" (hymn 4), "long–eyed" (hymn 5), "she of the fine forehead" (hymn 8), "Kōtai of the curly black tresses" (hymn 9), "glossy–haired Kōtai" (hymn 12), "whose eyebrows arch like a bow" (hymn 13), and finally as *viyaṉ* (hymn 13), which may be translated as "she of excellence."

The corpus of poems composed by Āṇṭāḷ's adoptive father, Viṣṇucitta, contain no direct reference to his daughter. However, two of the hymns in the third decade of his *Periya Tirumoḻi*, spoken in the voice of a lamenting mother whose daughter is in love with Kṛṣṇa, are full of nuances and lend themselves to the suggestion that Periyāḻvār composed these verses with his own daughter in mind. For those among the devout who believe in the legend of Āṇṭāḷ's life, such an assumption would not be far wrong:

I have but one daughter–
the world hailed my great fortune.
I raised her as if
she were the goddess Śrī–
lotus–eyed Māl took her away.[11]

However, Viṣṇucitta states clearly in the signature verse to this hymn that he is not speaking in his own voice:

The sorrowful words spoken by the mother
were sung by the *paṭṭar*
of prosperous Putuvai.

The Fame of Āṇṭāḷ: Art, Taniyaṉs, Inscriptions, Literary Works

A tenth century bronze image of Āṇṭāḷ, revealing a sensuous modelling (see cover), stands within the shrine of the Śrīvilliputtūr temple. It displays a heightened awareness of form, with a supple treatment of the planes of the body and a smooth unpronounced curve of the stomach that is typical of bronzes of the workshop of Chola Queen Śembiyan Mahādevī,[12] and it was probably produced around the year 970. The stylized bands of the ends of the lower garment as they rest upon her thigh, the treatment of the extra length of skirt which has been pleated to fall between her legs in folds, and the manner in which the necklaces rest between her breasts and encircle them are characteristic of this period of perfection. The worn condition of the bronze reflects centuries of ritual bathing and extensive worship; devotees, of course, only view the richly decorated image, draped with heavy gold saris and adorned with sumptuous jewelry and fragrant flower garlands.

In the same tenth century, *ācārya* Uyyakkoṇṭār of Śrīraṅkam wrote two single verses known as *taniyan̲s* (singletons) as a prelude to Āṇṭāḷ's *Tiruppāvai*, glorifying the song and its author. Both *taniyan̲s* refer to the event central to her legend, Viṣṇu's acceptance of the garland she had worn.

Let us meditate upon
Āṇṭāḷ of Putuvai
where swans wander in the fields—
the lady who gave
to the lord of Araṅkam
this polished garland of songs,
the fine poems of the *Tiruppāvai*
which lend themselves to melody—
the lady who gave to the lord
the garland of flowers
she had worn.

The second *taniyan̲* links the *Tiruppāvai* to her later work *Nācciyār Tirumoḻi*, and contains a reference to its first hymn in which Āṇṭāḷ requests the god of love, Man̲matha, to unite her with the lord of Vēṅkaṭa:

O creeper of radiance
who gave what she had worn—
you of bangled hands
who sang of the ancient *pāvai*
conferring blessings on all who heard—
you sought the lord of Vēṅkaṭa,
prayed to be taken to him.
Grant that we never ignore
your great words.

A century and a half later, *ācārya* Parāśara Paṭṭar composed a Sanskrit *taniyan̲* for the *Tiruppāvai*, alluding to its nineteenth song in which Āṇṭāḷ and her companions rouse Kṛṣṇa who is sleeping with his head resting against Nappiṉṉai's breasts:

She awakened Kṛṣṇa
who slumbered beneath
the rising breasts of Nīlādevī.
She enjoys the lord
whom she enslaved
with her discarded
garland of flowers.
She reveals to others
that which is revealed
in a hundred *śrutis.*
To that revered Kōtai
our obeisance.
May her fame live on
until the end of time.

The *taniyaṉs* of the *Nācciyār Tirumoḻi* are of a later date than those that preface the *Tiruppāvai.* The earliest, composed in the twelfth or thirteenth century by Tirukaṇṇamaṅkai Āṇṭāṉ, visualized Āṇṭāḷ as an incarnation of Bhūdevī, hence a fitting companion for Śrī Lakṣmi:

Gracious companion
to the lovely goddess
whose seat
is the fresh blown lotus—
Beautiful peacock,
queen of Mallināṭu,
softness incarnate,
radiant light
of the cowherds
of southern Putuvai—
Fitting consort to the cowherd lord.

This verse prefaces the *Nācciyār Tirumoḻi* in all printed versions of the four thousand verses of the Aḻvārs, the *Nālāyira Tivya Pirapantam.*

A second *taniyaṉ*, more intimate in tone, alludes pointedly to the content of the hymns of the *Nācciyār Tirumoḻi.* This anonymous verse, included only in certain printed versions of the *Tirumoḻi,* commences with a reference to its seventh hymn which Āṇṭāḷ addressed to the conch shell that was fortunate enough to be held in Viṣṇu's hand and raised to his lips when he wished to blow it:

She queried
the conch shell
about the flavor and fragrance
of the red lips
of the lord of illusion.
She dressed
her glossy tresses
with the glorious garland
of *katampa* flowers
intended for the lord of Araṅkam.
That soft–spoken parakeet
of the forest groves,
esteemed lady,
queen of southern Mallināṭu—
Forever
our refuge will be
her holy feet.

Inscriptions indicate that by the early twelfth century the fame of Āṇṭāḷ was so well established that a garden at Śrīraṅkam was named after her as "Kōtai Āṇṭāḷ Tirunanta-vanam" or "Sacred Pleasure Garden of Kōtai Āṇṭāḷ". The epigraph giving us this information[13] is dated in the eighth year of King Vikrama Chola, or 1126 A.D. At Śrīvilliputtūr, Āṇṭāḷ's divine status was never in doubt. A lengthy inscription in the temple,[14] dated in the year 1454, takes the form of a love letter from Viṣṇu to Āṇṭāḷ and testifies both to Āṇṭāḷ's high status and to the renown of her poems. The "letter" quotes numerous extracts, even entire verses from the *Nācciyār Tirumoḻi,* including its most dramatic verse from hymn thirteen in which Āṇṭāḷ vows to pluck out her breasts and fling them at the lord if he does not come to her. A few phrases from the better known *Tiruppāvai* are also quoted. The "love letter" concludes by declaring that the lord, well–pleased with Āṇṭāḷ, ordains that the honors accorded to him should be extended also to her.

The legend of Āṇṭāḷ spread beyond the Tamil country, and the Vijayanagar Emperor Kṛṣṇadevarāya (1510–1529), an ardent Vaiṣṇava and apparently a special devotee of Āṇṭāḷ, wrote the Telegu poem *Āmuktamālyada*[15], which revolves around her life. The Telegu version follows the Sanskrit hagiography, *Divyasūricaritam*, in carrying the story one step beyond Āṇṭāḷ's miraculous merger with the Śrīraṅkam stone symbol of her beloved, and relates that in deference to the wishes of Periyāḻvār, the lord of Śrīraṅkam traveled to Śrīvilliputtūr, where he ceremonially married Āṇṭāḷ.

The Viṣṇu Legend in Āṇṭāḷ's Poetry

It is clear from both the *Tiruppāvai* and the *Nācciyār Tirumoḻi* that Āṇṭāḷ's chosen god is Kṛṣṇa the cowherd lord, beloved of the *gopīs* (cowherdesses); however, the emphasis in the two works is somewhat different. The thirty verses of the *Tiruppāvai* are set in Āyarpāṭi or Gokula itself, and Āṇṭāḷ presents us with an early morning pastoral scene with buffaloes grazing, cows lowing, and Āyarpāṭi maidens churning butter. Kṛṣṇa is specifically identified as a cowherd's son, and as one born into a cowherd clan. He is extolled as the radiant light of the cowherd clan, one who dwells on the banks of the sacred Yamunā, and lord of Maturai of the north. References abound to his many exploits as Kṛṣṇa—his destruction of the demoness Pūtanā, cart–demon (Śakata), horse–demon (Keśin), crane–demon (Baka), calf elephant (Kuvalayāpīda), and finally evil king (Kaṃsa). While the verses of the *Tiruppāvai* undoubtedly revolve around Kṛṣṇa, it is apparent that Viṣṇu and Kṛṣṇa are not sharply differentiated in Kōtai's awareness. On occasion Kṛṣṇa is visualized in his cosmic form as one who slumbers upon his serpent in the milky ocean (verses 2 and 6), or as the child who lay upon the banyan leaf (verse 26). Two of his incarnations are extolled, as *Vāmana*, the dwarf who spanned and measured the worlds (verses 3, 17, 24), and as Rāma who destroyed the king of Laṅkā (verses 12, 24). These references, however, are overshadowed by the setting of Kṛṣṇa's Āyarpāṭi in which the entire *Tiruppāvai* episode is re-enacted.

In the *Nācciyār Tirumoḻi*, the situation is somewhat more complex, and the geographical location of the fourteen hymns remains uncertain. Only hymn two in which the *gopī* girls build sandcastles, and hymn three in which they plead with Kṛṣṇa to give them back the clothes he has stolen while they were bathing, may be seen as occurring in Āyarpāṭi. The action of the remaining hymns takes place in an unspecified location in South India, most likely in Āṇṭāḷ's home town of Śrīvilliputtūr itself, while hymn nine is specifically located in Māliruñcōlai, modern Aḻakarkoil, some twenty-five miles from Maturai. The central figure of Āṇṭāḷ's *Nācciyār Tirumoḻi* hymns too is undoubtedly Kṛṣṇa. Yet hymn eight, in which Āṇṭāḷ sends the clouds as her messengers of love, is dedicated in its entirety to the lord of the Vēṅkaṭa hill (Tirupati), while hymn eleven, in which Āṇṭāḷ exclaims that the lord has taken all from her, extols in each of its verses the lord of Araṅkam (Śrīraṅkam). In addition, an entire series of verses in the *Nācciyār Tirumoḻi* contain references both to an aspect of Kṛṣṇa and to one of the manifestations or incarnations of Viṣṇu.[16] A verse which commences by addressing her lord as Govinda (cowherd lord), proceeds to describe him as one who spanned the earth and measured it, a reference to Viṣṇu's dwarf avatar also known as Trivikrama (hymn 2, verse 9). A verse sung to Kṛṣṇa perched high up on a tree with the garments of the *gopīs*, addresses him as lord of Laṅkā or Rāma. Displaying her sense of humor Āṇṭāḷ, as one of the *gopīs*, tells Kṛṣṇa that he is indeed the king of monkeys (hymn 3, verse 4), implying that they now understand why Hanumān and his clan followed him in his incarnation as Rāma. A third verse speaks of Govinda (cowherd lord) who lives on the hill of Vēṅkaṭa or Tirupati (hymn 8, verse 3), and a fourth speaks of the lord of Araṅkam (Śrīraṅkam) who claimed Rukminī as his own in the Kṛṣṇa avatar (hymn 11, verse 9). Yet another verse which refers to the cowherd lord who dances with the waterpots, describes him as reclining in Kuṭantai (Kumpakōṇam) and also speaks of him as having slumbered upon a banyan leaf (hymn 13, verse 2). Examples of this type could be multiplied to demonstrate that Viṣṇu and Kṛṣṇa existed side by side in Āṇṭāḷ's consciousness.

A rough count of references to Viṣṇu reveals fifteen verses that speak of the lord of Vēṅkaṭa, eleven of the lord of Māliruñcōlai, ten of the lord of Araṅkam, ten of the lord of the milky ocean. Of the incarnations, Trivikrama (mentioned fifteen times) and Rāma (ten allusions) were favorites, although references are made to Varāha and Narasimha as well.

Yet it is Kṛṣṇa (sixty references, which is roughly the sum total of her visualization of other forms of Viṣṇu) who is undoubtedly the source of Āṇṭāḷ's inspiration and the central figure of her verses. While this is evident throughout the *Nācciyār Tirumoḻi*, it is perhaps clearest in the last few songs of this work. In the twelfth song, Āṇṭāḷ appeals to her family and friends, telling them of her determination to go to her beloved, and asking them to send her to the land of her lord. In successive verses she asks them to take her to a range of sites associated with the Kṛṣṇa legend—to Maturai (Mathura) where Kṛṣṇa fought the Mallas, to Āyarpāṭi (Tamil for Gokula in Vṛindāvan), to the threshold of Nandagōpa's house, to Bhaktavilōcana where the cowherds received sacrifical food, to the tree at Bāndiram where Baladeva fought the demon Pralamba, to Govardhana where Kṛṣṇa held aloft the mountain, and to the city of Dvārka where he reigned as king. The signature verse sums up the Kṛṣṇa legend, stating that Āṇṭāḷ beseeched her relatives to take her to the dwelling places of her lord, "beginning with famed Maturai/ending with Dvārka." In the climactic thirteenth hymn where a desperate Āṇṭāḷ threatens to pluck out her breasts and fling them at the lord to quench the fire of anguish within her, she addresses him as lord of Govardhana, again a reference to cowherd Kṛṣṇa. In the last hymn, quiet finally descends upon her as evidenced by the peaceful detachment of its question-and-answer mode. In each verse Āṇṭāḷ queries if anyone has seen her lord, and in each verse the answer she receives, refers to her cowherd lord, "we saw him there in Vṛindāvan."

The Pāvai Vow[17]

The *Tiruppāvai* revolves around the purely Tamil tradition of the *pāvai* vow of the month of Mārkaḷi (mid–December to mid–January), associated in earlier literature, however, with the succeeding month of Tai (mid–January to mid–February). The vow was undertaken by young unmarried girls who, throughout the month, bathed at dawn in the cold waters of a river or pond to secure the blessing of a happy married life. In his discussion of *pāvai* ritual, Norman Cutler draws attention to a reference to the practice in one of the hymns of the *Paripāṭal*,[18] a work assigned to the sixth or seventh century. The poem, dedicated to the Vaikai river, describes young girls bathing at the chilly hour of dawn, drying their clothes beside the fires kindled by brahmins along the river banks, and addressing the Vaikai river, praying for a fine lover and many children. In this work, and in several others of an early date, the vow is undertaken in the month of Tai. Cutler suggests that the shift to Mārkaḷi, evidenced in Āṇṭāḷ's *Tiruppāvai*, is the result of a shift from the lunar to the solar calendar, which has since been the norm in Tamil-speaking areas of South India.

One assumes that it was from a variety of such sources belonging to the early Caṅkam anthologies, all of which reflect the popularity of the *pāvai* ritual, generally in a secular context, that Āṇṭāḷ found material for her *Tiruppāvai* poems which she adapted to the worship of Kṛṣṇa. Śaiva saint Māṇikkavācakar probably drew on the same sources for his *Tiruvempāvai* in which the god addressed is Śiva. A Jain *pāvai* song of early date, belonging perhaps to the eighth century and addressing the deity as Arivan̲, has survived as a single verse only, but it contains the essential components of the *pāvai* theme.[19] It provides a glimpse into the adaptation of the theme to a religion that stresses world renunciation, and it also highlights the great popularity of the *pāvai* tradition in Tamil-speaking areas of South India.

The only Sanskrit work to speak of the *pāvai* theme is the *Bhāgavata Purāṇa* which, we shall see, was compiled in the period following the Tamil saints. The Tamil *pāvai* vow, unknown to the rest of India, finds mention in one relatively brief, though important passage in the tenth book. We are told that in the first month of the winter, the maidens of Gokula took a vow to worship the goddess Kātyāyani, who is also addressed as Bhadrakālī, in order to gain Kṛṣṇa as their spouse. Bathing at dawn in the waters of the Yamunā, they fashioned an image of the goddess from the sand along the river bank and worshipped her with offerings of flowers, fruit, rice, incense and lamps.[20] It would appear that the authors of the *Bhāgavata Purāṇa* felt that they could not entirely omit reference to the popular and widely prevalent Tamil *pāvai* vow. Yet, since their audience would not relate to it or understand its significance, they played down the theme.

An integral part of *pāvai* ritual is bathing in the waters of a river, tank, pond or lake. Māṇikkavācakar's *Tiruvempāvai*[21] commences with a series of verses in which young girls are aroused from sleep to go bathe in the waters; it proceeds with stanzas that speak repeatedly of the pond, its surroundings, and the playful bathing of the maidens. The Śaiva poet describes the girls splashing around in the pond and plunging into its waters (verse 11), tells us that the pond is filled with lotuses (verse 12), that the waters cover the breasts of the maidens, that flocks of cranes come to the pond which is fringed with dark water lilies, and he speaks of the musical jingle of armlets and anklets as the girls jump playfully, scooping up the foaming waters (verse 13).

Āṇṭāḷ's *Tiruppāvai* presents a striking contrast to this water imagery. While Āṇṭāḷ too allocates ten verses to arousing maidens to go bathe in the waters, the group never go to a pond or lake. Instead they go to the home of Kṛṣṇa's adoptive parents, Nandagōpa and Yaśodā, and awaken them; next they proceed to awaken Kṛṣṇa's cowherd wife, Nappiṉṉai, and beg her to awaken her lord. The maidens then praise Kṛṣṇa and ask him to "bathe us now in the waters" (*ippōtē emmai nīrāṭṭu*). It is clear that Āṇṭāḷ's bathing (*nirāṭal*) has a wealth of significance beyond the simple literal bathing suggested by the *pāvai* vow.[22] Kṛṣṇa (the divine) is envisaged as a *tīrtha* or sacred purifying waters, and the "diving deep" is somewhat akin to that envisaged by the term "Āḻvār" as "one who dives deep (into the divine)." Only in this context does the absence, in the *Tiruppāvai*, of any description of bathing in physical waters, be it pond, tank, or river, make logical sense. Only then may we understand Āṇṭāḷ's request that Kṛṣṇa should "bathe us now in the waters," to be understood as the divine waters of Kṛṣṇa's grace. As an aside, it may also be mentioned that *nirāṭal* (bathing in the waters) and *cuṉaiāṭal* (bathing in a hill tank) are both euphemisms for sexual union. And sexual imagery, as we know, has long been used in Hinduism to describe the union of the individual soul with the universal soul. As Dennis Hudson phrases it, the goal of the maidens is "intimate service to Krishna which may mean sexual union with him, euphemistically referred to as a bath; 'bathing in Krishna', one might say, is the goal—a relationship of service so total that there are no limitations whatsoever."[23]

A parallel to Āṇṭāḷ's vision of *nirāṭal* as bathing in the sacred purifying waters of the divine, may be seen in a hymn of the seventh century Śaiva saint Appar. A song extolling Śiva of the shrine of Tiruvānaikkā, near Śrīraṅkam, has the following invocatory refrain to each of its ten verses:

> O infinitude of fresh, cool waters—
> I plunge, I revel.[24]

Also significant in the context of the *pāvai* vow is Āṇṭāḷ's assertion, in the very first verse of *Tiruppāvai*, that the lord himself will give the young maidens the *parai*. In several succeeding verses (8, 10, 16, 24, 25, 27–30) she states that they have gone to the lord to receive the *parai* that he promised them. The word *parai* literally means "drum," and the drum sound, signifying creativity and prosperity, is considered auspicious. The beating of the drum initiates all sacred as well as secular ritual, and it is believed that sacred power can be transmitted through the sound of the drum. In the context of the *Tiruppāvai*, the transmission of potency through the sound of the drum may be equated with the transmission of divine grace. In its symbolic meaning, the giving of the *parai* signifies the bestowal upon the devotee of all her desires; it can also be interpreted as the joy of being with the lord and the honor of serving him. The bestowal of the *parai* also indicates the successful completion of the *pāvai* vow. For Āṇṭāḷ, of course, to obtain Kṛṣṇa's grace, and to be one with him, is the only goal, the only heart's desire. Āṇṭāḷ's *nirāṭal* (bathing in Krsna) precedes the bestowal of the *parai* (nearness to Kṛṣṇa, fulfillment).

The words *ēl ōr empāvāy*, which occur as the refrain to each of the thirty songs of the *Tiruppāvai*, as indeed of

Māṇikkavācakar's Śaiva *Tiruvempāvai* and also the Jain *pāvai* poem, have posed a problem of interpretation to all who have tried to translate or study these poems. Some translators have totally ignored the refrain[25]; we feel it deserves a place since it supplies the very word form that occurs in the title of these poems. The word *pāvai* means a young girl or woman, an image or doll, and also the vow of *pāvai*.[26] In the course of the thirty *Tiruppāvai* songs, ignoring for the moment the refrain, the word is used in the first sense of young girl (song 13) and in its last meaning of vow (song 2). In translating the refrain to read, "Fulfill, O song of our vow", we have been influenced by several factors. Not the least is the fact that the refrain, sung by Āṇṭāḷ in the context of Āyarpāṭi and Kṛṣṇa, is used in identical form by both a Śaiva poet and a Jain author. It seems to us that the refrain must necessarily be applicable to all three works. Common to all three is the fact that the songs are sung by women, that young girls are awakened from their sleep, called to bathe in the waters and then praise the lord (Śiva in the case of Māṇikkavācakar, and Arivaṉ in the case of the Jain poet). Āṇṭāḷ's bathing, as we have seen, falls into a unique category. Common to the *pāvai* songs, in symbolic terms, is the awakening of those oblivious of the divine, their purification (bathing), followed by beseeching the lord for his grace. The phrase *empāvāy* seems to mean "O our vow" as also "O our song" (*pāvai* songs having become a separate category), with the word *pāvāy* being in the vocative case. The words *ēl* and *ōr* seem to be mere expletives. We have added the request "Fulfill" because it seemed to us that this is the unspoken prayer of the refrain. "Fulfill, O song of our vow" appears suitable also as refrains to the Śaiva and Jain poems. We might add here that such a translation of the refrain would accord with the interpretation of the celebrated thirteenth century commentator Periyavāccāṉ Piḷḷai[27] who suggests the meanings of "vow" and "song" for *empāvāy*, and explains *ēl* and *ōr* as expletives.

An alternative interpretation of the refrain would be "O our lady of the vow".[28] In this meaning, the phrase *ēl ōr empāvāy* could be considered as compact with the two meanings of image (translated here as lady) as well as the vow itself. We have already alluded to the *pāvai* vow mentioned in the

Bhāgavata Purāṇa, in which an image (*pāvai*) of Kātyāyani was made out of sand and worshiped as part of the vow (*pāvai*). Taking this dual meaning into consideration seems to be one way to interpret Āṇṭāḷ's repetitive phrase. In support of such an interpretation is the fact that the *Paripāṭal*, already alluded to, speaks of the bathing of the girls as *ampāvāṭal*. While this phrase has generally been translated as "bathing with their mothers" or "bathing in the presence of their mothers," scholars agree that the word *ampā* could be a reference to the goddess, and that *ampāvāṭal* may refer to the bathing vow performed for the goddess.[29] Our reason for suggesting that this interpretation of the refrain may not be the most suitable one, lies partly in the fact that the idea of the goddess seems less appropriate in the case of Śiva and the Jīna, and partly because Āṇṭāḷ's own verses seem to suggest a total absorption in Kṛṣṇa to the neglect of all else, including a goddess of the vow. If it was Nappiṉṉai that Āṇṭāḷ visualized in this role and intended to address in the refrain, then we have to find an alternative goddess for the phrase when it is used in a Śaiva or Jain context.

Intriguing evidence exists of the importance in Thailand of Āṇṭāḷ's *Tiruppāvai* and Māṇikkavācakar's *Tiruvempāvai*. In Bangkok, during the month of Tai, a festival known officially as *Triyambāvāy Tripāvāy* (*Tiruvempāvai Tiruppāvai*), and more popularly as *Lo Jin Ja* or "pulling the swing" is celebrated. Apparently, Thai brahmin priests recite two verses of Māṇikkavācakar's *Tiruvempāvai* during the festival.[30] The date at which these poems reached Thailand, and the reason for their adoption in that distant country, are matters for further investigation.

Āṇṭāḷ's Poetry and the Bhāgavata Purāṇa

It appears certain that the *Bhāgavata Purāṇa*, which is the main text for the legend of Viṣṇu, is later than Āḻvār poetry since it makes selective use of themes from the poems of these saints. The relationship between Tamil Āḻvār poetry and the Sanskrit *Bhāgavata Purāṇa* has been explored by Friedhelm Hardy,[31] who points out that the *Purāṇa* was composed in South India in the ninth century, and that it combined themes from the poems of the Āḻvārs (600–900) with the input of the northern Sanskrit *Brahmā* and *Viṣṇu Purāṇas* (500–700). From the perspective of Āṇṭāḷ's poetry, an important reason for concluding that the songs of the Āḻvārs must predate the *Bhāgavata Purāṇa* is the fact that two episodes prominent in the *Purāṇa* are not mentioned by Āṇṭāḷ. The celebrated *rasa* dance of Kṛṣṇa with the *gopīs*, and the theme of their intense longing for Kṛṣṇa combined with the pain of separation from him once he leaves Gokula for Mathurā, are given specific treatment in independent chapters of the *Bhāgavata Purāṇa*. These are taken, as Hardy points out,[32] from the narrative in the Sanskrit *Brahmā* and *Viṣṇu Purāṇas*. If Āṇṭāḷ had known of these two Kṛṣṇa themes through the *Bhāgavata Purāṇa*, she would undoubtedly have made use of them in her poems. With Kṛṣṇa as her chosen lord, and the anguish of separation as the personal theme of her *Nācciyār Tirumoḻi*, Āṇṭāḷ would surely have made reference to the agony of the *gopīs* when Kṛṣṇa departs.[33]

Another theme which finds no place in the *Bhāgavata Purāṇa* is the *ciṟṟil* or sandcastle song; to this mode Āṇṭāḷ devotes a whole hymn in which a group of young girls beseech Kṛṣṇa not to break the playhouses they have built. *Ciṟṟil* songs are a Tamil tradition already used in Caṅkam poetry of the first few centuries A.D., in which it is not connected with Kṛṣṇa (*Kalittokai* 51).[34] Āṇṭāḷ used the *ciṟṟil* mode in the ten verses of her second *Nācciyāṛ* hymn, speaking of the simple emotions of little girls in love with child Kṛṣṇa. The mode was used briefly in connection with Kṛṣṇa (but in a single verse only) by other Āḻvārs too including Tirumaṅkai, Nammāḻvār and Periyāḻvār. The *Bhāgavata Purāṇa*, written in Sanskrit for a northern audience, has omitted the *ciṟṟil* theme, presumably because it is a typically southern motif; having no counterpart in the north, it would fail to evoke response. In a similar manner, we have seen that the popular southern *pāvai* theme was utilized only in minimal fashion in the *Bhāgavata Purāṇa*.

It would appear that the author, or authors, of the *Bhāgavata Purāṇa* selected certain themes from the poems of the Tamil saints and, combining these with their Sanskrit sources, produced what remains the authoritative version of the story of Viṣṇu, in which the exploits of Kṛṣṇa play a major role.

Āṇṭāḷ and Tamil Caṅkam Poetry

Being part of the southern milieu, the Tamil bhakti poets, including Āṇṭāḷ, quite naturally drew upon the earlier traditions of Caṅkam literature.[35] For example, Āṇṭāḷ speaks of the *teṉṟal* (southern breeze) and *tiṅkaḷ* (moon) adding to the sorrows of love (*Nācciyār Tirumoḻi*, hymn 5, verse 10)—an age-old theme of Tamil poetry. She refers to the concept of *peruntiṇai* or excessive love which breaks the rules of social decorum, when she speaks of word getting round that she left her home and family and went to her beloved (*Nācciyār Tirumoḻi*, hymn 12, verse 3). She displays an intensive awareness of nature, which is a hallmark of Caṅkam poetry as is evident from A. K. Ramanujan's very choice of title for his translations of those classical poems—"The Interior Landscape".[36] Nature and human emotions mirror each other in the Caṅkam poems, in which some two hundred varieties of plants and flowers are named, described and used to evoke human relationships.[37]

While Āṇṭāḷ made extensive use of images of nature, such imagery was generally not used as a vehicle for subtle implied meaning (*uḷḷuṟai*), as is invariably the case in Caṅkam poems. In fact, when commentators strive to find an inner meaning for Āṇṭāḷ's nature imagery, their efforts often appear forced. Āṇṭāḷ's use of images from nature seems to present a more direct appeal. In her longing for the lord, she addresses verses to the jasmine, the *kōvai* creeper, the climbing lily, water lotuses, swarms of bees, dark rain clouds, the deep ocean. She especially chides the koelbirds, peacocks, *karuviḷai* blossoms, bilberries and dark *kāyā* flowers (*Nācciyār Tirumoḻi*, hymn 9, verse 4):

You five great sinners,
dwellers in this lush grove
of Māliruñcōlai—
koelbirds, peacocks,
deep blue *karuviḷai* blossoms,
fresh black bilberries,
purple *kāyā* flowers—
What avails you

the dark color
of my lord?

She compares herself to the milky *erukku* leaf and states that if the lord does not come to her, she too will wither and fall in the dry season of summer (*Nācciyār Tirumoḻi*, hymn 8, verse 8). In a grove full of the flowering buttercup trees sacred to her Lord Viṣṇu, she compares her unfulfilled existence to the worthless cassia blossom sacred to the god Śiva (*Nācciyār Tirumoḻi*, hymn 9, verse 9):

In the hilly grove of Māliruñcōlai
where the glorious buttercup blooms,
I live unprofitable days
hanging in vain
like golden garlands of cassia.

The parallels that exist between the earlier *puṟam*, or war poems of Caṅkam literature, and the later bhakti poems have been highlighted by Norman Cutler who demonstrates how the poet–to–king relationship was used by the bhakti poets who replaced the king with god.[38] This source of poetic inspiration for the Āḻvārs and Nāyaṉmārs was indeed a major one. "Past traditions and borrowings are thus reworked into bhakti,"[39] but, as Ramanujan phrases it, the poet "does not think about tradition, he thinks with it, within it. Tradition in this precise sense. provides him his material, his medium, his model, his universe of signifiers."[40]

Āṇṭāḷ's Prosody

While my focus is mainly on Āṇṭāḷ's bhakti and mysticism, it would be of interest to briefly consider her poetry from the point of view of Tamil metrical structure. Tamil meter (*yāppu*) is based on metrical syllables (*acai*) which are put together in complex ways, and in a variety of combinations to produce metrical feet (*cīr*). Āṇṭāḷ used five different types of meters in the fourteen poems of her *Nācciyār Tirumoḻi*. The *aṟucīr āciriya viruttam* (six metrical feet) is seen in songs 1, 3, 12, 13, 14; the *eḻucīr āciriya viruttam* (seven metrical feet) in song five; *kali viruttam* (four metrical feet and four lines per stanza) in songs 2, 4, 6, 7, 8, 9; *kali nilai tuṟai* (five metrical feet) in song ten; and *koccaka kalippā* (four metrical feet and an unlimited number of lines) in song eleven. It is this last meter than Āṇṭāḷ used in all thirty songs of her Tiruppāvai.

The first song of the *Nācciyār Tirumoḻi* uses the *aṟucīr* meter based on six metrical feet, as seen in its first line given below:

1 2 3 4 5 6
taioru tiṅkaḷum taraiviḷakkit taṇmaṇ ṭalamiṭṭu mācimuṉṉāḷ

Through the month of Tai
I swept the ground before my house,
made sacred mandalas of fine sand.
The month of Māci has begun.

It may be noted that often, as in the word *maṇṭala* (mandala) seen in *cīrs* four and five, one half of a word ends one metrical foot, while the other half commences the next foot.[41] A similar occurrence is evident in the words *naraṉē* and *makaṉ* in the following example of *kali viruttam*, which consists of four metrical feet in a stanza of four lines only, from the opening of the second song:

1 2 3 4
nāmamāyiram ēttaniṉra nārāyaṇānara ṉēuṉṉai

1 2 3 4
māmitaṉmaka ṉākapeṟṟāl emakkuvātai tavirumē

Lord praised by a thousand names,
O Nara, O Nārāyaṇa,
you took birth as Yaśodā's son—
we cannot escape your pranks.

A typical feature of all Āṇṭāḷ's poems, as of Tamil poetry in general, is initial rhyme (*etukai*) that occurs in the second syllable of each line of a stanza:

karuppūram nāṟumō kamalappū nāṟumō
tiruppavaḷac cevvāytāṉ tittit tirukkumō
maruppocitta mātavaṉtaṉ vāycuvaiyum nāṟṟamum
viruppuṟṟuk kētkiṉṟēṉ colāḻi veṇcaṅkē

camphor does–it–smell lotus bloom does–it–smell
sacred–coral-red–lips-themselves sweet–will–it–be
tusk–who–broke–Mādhavaṉ his lips taste and smell
eagerness–with ask I tell deep sea white conch.

Do they smell of camphor
or of the lotus bloom?
Do they taste sweet
his sacred lips of coral hue?
O white conch
from the fathomless sea,
I long to know,
tell me the taste,
the fragrance
of the lips of Mādhavaṉ
who broke the elephant's tusk.

The underlined words, or part of a word, result in the production of the initial rhyme, with the second syllable *ru* being the key letter.

Āṇṭāḷ's Tamil is, in her own words, pure Tamil, *tūya* Tamil (*Nācciyār Tirumoḻi*, song 6, verse 11), or *ceṉ* Tamil (*Nācciyār Tirumoḻi*, song 9, verse 10). The admixture of Sanskrit words, such as *maṇḍala, bālaka, toraṇa, devar,* is at a minimum and accounts for no more than 10 per cent of her entire vocabulary. She does not use Sanskrit words to achieve special effects as was done frequently in later days.

Āṇṭāḷ and Tamil Bhakti Poetry

In a section entitled "A New Poetics?" contained in the *Afterword* to a translation of Nammāḻvār's verses, A. K. Ramanujan has provided us with a lucid and explicit analysis of the elements that characterize Tamil bhakti poetry and distinguish it from both earlier classical Tamil and from the Sanskrit tradition.[42] I can do no better than to echo his points here, highlighting those that are particularly applicable to Āṇṭāḷ's poetic vision. Also full of insights and most pertinent to our discussion is Norman Cutler's analysis of the rhetorical structure of bhakti poems in his recent work on the poetry of the saints,[43] in which he speaks of the variety of relationships possible between poet, god and audience.

Three main factors may be seen to distinguish bhakti poetry from both classical Tamil literature and classical Sanskrit poetics. While all poetry aims at the creation of an aesthetic impact, the bhakti poet gives importance, in addition, to the religious purpose or the practical end that the poem can serve, a factor that has no place in the classical tradition. The last verse of the *Tiruppāvai*, and of each of the fourteen hymns of the *Nācciyār Tirumoḻi*, are signature verses in which Āṇṭāḷ announces to her audience the benefits to be achieved by reciting her verses:

Those who repeat
this garland of Tamil verses
will attain
the feet of the lord.

(*Nācciyār Tirumoḻi*, hymn 1, verse 10)

Those who recite
this pure garland of ten Tamil verses
will live in joy
and bear fine and noble children.

(*Nācciyār Tirumoḻi*, hymn 6, verse 11)
The Wedding Hymn

Those who repeat these verses
will never drown
in the sea of sorrow.

(*Nācciyār Tirumoḻi*, hymn 13, verse 10)

This reward will be theirs
who chant together
faultlessly
this Tamil garland of thirty songs—
the grace of Tirumāl
will be upon them—
lord of limitless wealth,
of holy countenance and lotus eyes,
whose four great shoulders

rise high as mountains.
They will live in joy
for ever more.

(*Tiruppāvai*, song 30)

Āṇṭāḷ's hymns were intended for a specific audience with whom she shared her god, her rapturous absorption in that god, and the agony of separation from him. In the course of time, due mainly to the fine quality of Āṇṭāḷ's poetry, her restricted audience became wide and general.

The second distinguishing feature of the bhakti tradition is the lack of dichotomy between the poet and the speaker, who are generally the same person; the poet seems ever present. Both the Sanskrit classical poem, Kālidāsa's *Mēghadūta* or "Cloud Messenger," and the Āḻvār messenger poems express similar emotions of love and longing for the beloved. In classical Sanskrit, however, it is the exiled *yakṣa* who sends the cloud as his messenger of love, and not the poet Kālidāsa. The poet and the speaker of the verses are two different persons—the dichotomy is clear and pronounced. By contrast, in bhakti poetry, the speaker, the sender of the message, is the poet himself. Śaiva child saint Campantar himself sends birds as messengers to Śiva, lord of Tōṇipuram; Āṇṭāḷ herself sends the koelbirds, the rain clouds, even the ocean as messengers to Lord Viṣṇu. Bhakti poetry expresses the inner need and the emotional state of the poet who is quite overtly the speaker.

In his study of bhakti poetry, Cutler divides the poems into five categories according to their rhetorical structure. In the first four categories, the poet is clearly the speaker, and he or she addresses variously the deity, a specific audience, his or her own heart, or an unspecified audience. The fifth category consists of poems in which neither speaker nor addressee is specified. Cutler points out that poems rhetorically most direct are at the core of Tamil bhakti,[44] and certainly one finds that Āṇṭāḷ herself is invariably the speaker in every one of her poems. In the *Tiruppāvai* she speaks either to her deity, Kṛṣṇa; or to a specific audience consisting of her companions or those close to Kṛṣṇa. In the hymns of *Nācciyār Tirumoḻi*, Āṇṭāḷ addresses only two songs directly to Kṛṣṇa (songs 2 and 3). Elsewhere she addresses birds, clouds, even the ocean, whom she wishes to send to Kṛṣṇa as her messengers of love. In certain poems, like song nine of the *Tirumoḻi*, individual verses are addressed to an unspecified audience.

In her narrative poems, Āṇṭāḷ frequently assumes roles suitable to express her personal experience and emotion. For example Āṇṭāḷ herself become a little girl building the sand houses that child Kṛṣṇa breaks (hymn 2); she herself assumes the guise of one of the *gopīs*, standing in the waters and begging Kṛṣṇa to throw down her clothes (hymn 3). She visualizes her own wedding to the lord (hymn 6), as is confirmed by the repeated refrain to each verse "I dreamt this dream, my friend."

The signature verses, as Cutler points out, operate in a different rhetorical structure from the rest of the poem, for in such verses the poet speaks of herself (himself) in the third person. In each of nine verses of hymn two of *Nācciyār Tirumoḻi*, Āṇṭāḷ plays the part of one of the little girls who have built sandcastles, herself begging the mischievous boy Kṛṣṇa not to break them:

> Naughty Śrīdhara,
> do not break
> our sandcastles.

In the tenth signature verse, however, Āṇṭāḷ refers to herself in the third person:

> Kōtai of Viṣṇucittaṉ, chief of Villiputtūr,
> home of those learned in the Vedas,
> has sung these verses
> telling of little *gopī* girls
> playing in the street,
> prattling
> and beseeching the lord
> who tasted the nectar of Sītā's lips
> not to destroy
> their castles of sand.
> Those who sing these Tamil verses
> will surely reach Vaikuṇṭa.

Cutler refers to such verses as "meta–poems," or poems about poems.[45]

A third and final point to be made regarding bhakti poetry concerns the widely held theory that, in contrast to the classical poet who works extensively at the creation of an aesthetic effect, the hallmark of the bhakti poet is her or his spontaneity. It is proposed that the bhakti poet composes without premeditation and that her (his) songs are the result of a spontaneous burst of inspiration.[46] Bhakti poems, it is suggested, are not entirely "emotion recollected in tranquillity", refined, polished, and then presented; they are often the immediate expression of strong emotion. While this ideal has been overstated, one sees the basis for such statements when considering, for instance, Āṇṭāḷ's impassioned and fearful threat in the penultimate hymn of *Nācciyār Tirumoḻi.* Having reached the depths in her emotional journey to her lord, Āṇṭāḷ feels betrayed and abandoned, and turns angrily upon him, expressing the despair of her heartbroken state:

> If I see the lord of Govardhana
> that looting thief,
> that plunderer,
> I shall pluck
> by their roots
> these useless breasts,
> I shall fling them
> at his chest,
> I shall cool
> the raging fire
> within me.
>
> (hymn 13, verse 8)

Āṇṭāḷ's spontaneity was the product of intense bhakti and *viraha tapa*, but at the same time, even in her state of heightened awareness, she remains a poet who adopted all the forms, metrical and modal, which were already part of the heritage of Tamil poetry. As Ramanujan points out, "without a repertoire of structures to rely on, there can be no spontaneity,"[47] even in what appears to be "free–seeming verse." One may consider the complex metrical structure of

Āṇṭāḷ's poems and the flawless manner in which the lines of
the verses hang together, commencing with studied initial
rhyming. In some instances Āṇṭāḷ's initial rhyming phrase is a
product of the joining of two words:

> pōyttīrtta māṭāte niṉṟapu ṇarmarutam
> cāyttīrttāṉ kaittalattē ērikku ṭikoṇṭu
> cēyttīrtta māyniṉṟa ceṅkaṇmāl taṉṉuṭaiya
> vāyttīrttam pāyntāṭa vallāyva lampuriyē

> having–gone–holy–water without–playing
>   standing–close–maruta
> bent–pulled palm–itself climbed–home–made
> holy site–as–standing red–eyed–Mal–his
> mount–water jump–play–you–can Valampuri–O.

> O Valampurī
> you did not search for holy sites
> you climbed into the lord's hand
> the holiest of sites
> You revel in the nectar
> of the lips
> of lotus–eyed Māl
> who dragged the maruta trees.

The rhyme occurs through the repetition of the word tīrtta
(tīrtha) meaning "holy site" or "holy waters;" while it seems to
appear in all four lines, the word in the second line is actually
cāyttu–īrttāṉ (bent–pulled). By the joining of these two words
(sandhi is as common a feature of Tamil as of Sanskrit), we get
cāyttīrttāṉ. Spontaneity, it seems, has perforce to be diluted to
make room for aesthetic effect. Āṇṭāḷ's "stunningly profound
poetic tapestries"[48] were woven by a skilled poet who had
considerable literary training and great facility with metrical
rhythm.

It may be pointed out in this context that bhakti poetry
tends to draw upon common speech and often uses colloquial
tones. Āṇṭāḷ brings in well–known sayings like ūmaiyarōṭu
ceviṭar vārttai, "the words you utter/are like the deaf/speaking
to the dumb" (Nācciyār Tirumoḻi, hymn 12, verse 1), or puṇṇil

puḷip peytār pōla or "your words sting/ like sour juice/poured upon an open wound" (*Nācciyār Tirumoḻi*, hymn 13, verse 1). She also uses colloquialisms like *talaiyiṭāte* (do not meddle), *vecavu uṇāte* (earn not scoldings), none of which would find a place in classical poetics. In addition, Āṇṭāḷ drew upon the common stock of popular songs, as did other saints, both Śaiva and Vaiṣṇava. Taking, for example, the *kūṭal* game played by young girls who wish to know if the object of their adoration loves them in return, Āṇṭāḷ adapted and reworked it into bhakti poetry (*Nācciyār Tirumoḻi*,hymn 4).

Āṇṭāḷ: Woman and Mystic

Treading the path of love, women saints have had a variety of relationships with their divine lord.[49] Many of them have been married women; to some the lord was a husband, to some beloved. Mahādeviyakkā (twelfth century), hopelessly and desperately in love with Śiva Mallikārjuna, was persuaded into marriage with a local chieftain. Her relationship with Śiva was ambiguous; she regarded him occasionally as her illegitimate lover and at other times as her only legitimate spouse. Eventually, against all social norm, she deserted her mortal husband in order to go in search of her lord. Mīrabai (sixteenth century) had, from early childhood, adored Kṛṣṇa as her prospective bridegroom; married against her wish to the prince of Chitor, her deep and intense preoccupation with Kṛṣṇa caused her to be persecuted by her in–laws and driven from her home. She traveled to Vṛindāvan where, feeling the presence of Kṛṣṇa, she spent her days in constant communion with him. Lallā of Kashmir (sixteenth century) was likewise married, but chose to regard her husband as her son in a previous birth; ultimately she renounced the world in order to follow the Śiva of her inner experience. Each of these women saints broke the bonds of social decorum, ignored their married status, and went forth in search of their divine spouse. Occasionally, however, as with sixth century Kāraikkāl Ammaiyār, the relationship between woman saint and divine lord was of a different nature. Once a happily married devotee, Kāraikkāl Ammaiyār gave herself up to Śiva upon being abandoned by her husband who was intimidated by her divine powers. Transformed at her own request into a skeletal ghoul, the Ammaiyār asked nothing more of Śiva than to be near him always, a devoted slave, singing his praises and watching him dance. Āṇṭāḷ is a rare instance of a woman saint who was yet a girl, on the threshold of womanhood and marriage, a fact that may explain her special mode of approach to her lord, and her candidly erotic phraseology in describing her longing for her divine lover.

Is it justified to make a distinction between Āṇṭāḷ the woman and Āṇṭāḷ the mystic? The temptation to suggest the existence of such a dichotomy disappears on a deeper analysis of her *Nācciyār Tirumoḻi* poems which reveals that woman and mystic invariably overlap. Āṇṭāḷ's whole life was an unfolding of bhakti; her physical womanhood cannot be seen in isolation from her mysticism.

Of Āṇṭāḷ's two works, the *Tiruppāvai* reveals the earlier phase of her spiritual journey. It was composed when Āṇṭāḷ was as yet happily treading the path, without doubt, fear or anguish, in the company of her young girl friends, searching strenuously for Kṛṣṇa and confident of finding him. Its songs describe the awakening of young girls in the early morning, and a call to them to join Āṇṭāḷ in the Mārkaḷi vow which enjoins a bath in the waters followed by worship and prayer. Āṇṭāḷ uses the *pāvai* vow, as well as the poetic form of the *pāvai* song, to disclose a progressive mystic journey in which one is aroused to a longing for the divine, made ready by a purificatory bath and finally, by prayer, aspiration and worship, made fit to receive his grace. Āṇṭāḷ and her companions never go to any physical waters for their bathing; they visualize a plunge into the holy *tīrtha* that is Kṛṣṇa.

The suggestion that the *Tiruppāvai* is the earlier work is reinforced by its position in the Vaiṣṇava sacred hymns, *Nālāyira Tivya Pirapantam*, in which it is followed by *Nācciyār Tirumoḻi*. Further support of this view comes from the fact, pointed out by Dennis Hudson, that the first word of *Tiruppāvai* is "mārkaḷi," while that of *Nācciyār Tirumoḻi* is "tai," the month that follows Mārkaḷi. Hudson suggests that Āṇṭāḷ organized her works by the calendar, and that "she meant the two works to feed into one another as do the months of the calendar."[50]

The *Nācciyār Tirumoḻi* reflects a later stage in Āṇṭāḷ's spiritual journey, revealing her as a woman who has once experienced the bliss of the lord's presence, but is now separated from him, spending her days in anguish at the separation. Kṛṣṇa is both the goal and the way to that goal, so that even in separation she finds an anguished joy in the ceaseless visualization of her lord and meditation on his various forms. Āṇṭāḷ's intense longing to be reunited with Kṛṣṇa and her changing moods of love, though often couched in the language of ordinary human love, is yet of a mystical supra–sensuous nature.

The feminine approach to the beloved is so compact of the element of total surrender that several men saints, including Nammāḻvār and Tirumaṅkai Āḻvār, composed songs in which they put themselves in the place of love–sick *gopīs* pining for Kṛṣṇa. What is unique, however, about Āṇṭāḷ's *Nācciyār Tirumoḻi* is the depth of what has been termed "Tamil anthropocentrism,"[51] evident in her ability to describe divine longing in terms of human love between woman and man. The very first hymn of the *Tirumoḻi*, addressed to Maṉmatha, god of love, in which Āṇṭāḷ beseeches Maṉmatha to unite her with her lord, contains several pointed references to her body, her breasts and her smooth stomach. One such reads:

Maṉmatha,
if you make
Trivikrama who spanned the worlds
caress me
with his sacred hands
my shapely breasts, my slender waist
will bring me fame on earth,
glory eternal.

(*Nācciyār Tirumoḻi*, hymn 1, verse 7)

In several hymns, Āṇṭāḷ addressing her beloved sounds like any young girl in love, imagining the various attractive qualities of the loved one and yearning to be near him. An instance of this is the verse quoted earlier in connection with Āṇṭāḷ's prosody, in which she envies the conch shell's nearness to Viṣṇu and its consequent intimacy with the lord.

When it comes to the expression of the anguish of separation, Āṇṭāḷ the woman seems to triumph over Āṇṭāḷ the mystic, as one who longs for a touch from the beloved, even though it be only the touch of something that has touched him.

Bring me his sacred basil
cool, lustrous, blue,
place it upon my glossy hair.
(*Nācciyār Tirumoḻi*, hymn 13, verse 2)

Bring me the cool nectar
from the mouth of his flute,
spread it upon my face
it will revive me
(*Nācciyār Tirumoḻi*, hymn 13, verse 5)

Bring me the dust
from the footprints
left by that insensitive lord–
smear it upon my body
that life may linger.
(*Nācciyār Tirumoḻi*, hymn 13, verse 6)

Again, in a slightly different context, Āṇṭāḷ expresses longing for the beloved in terms which sound purely physical. Addressing the clouds, she pleads:

Tell him I will survive
only if he will stay with me
for one day—
enter me
so as to wipe away
the saffron paste
adorning my breasts.
(*Nācciyār Tirumoḻi*, hymn 8, verse 7)

Later she speaks to the ocean, telling how the lord had entered her:

O great deep ocean,
the lord entered into you,

mixed and churned you,
deprived you of your nectar.
That Māyan entered into me too,
churned me,
drained me of my essence.

(*Nācciyār Tirumoḻi*, hymn 10, verse 9)

Yet, the mystic overtones are much too deep to be categorized as mere "anthropocentrism." The infinite invisible also "enters" and also "leaves its mark;" the divine entry "churns" and empties. The "I" of the mystic and the "I" of the young woman Āṇṭāḷ are inextricably merged.

Notes to Chapter One

1. Because she is a woman, it is sometimes held that Āṇṭāḷ is not technically an Āḻvār; however, she is usually referred to as one of the twelve.

2. See R. Nagaswamy, *Studies in Ancient Tamil Law and Society* (Madras : Tamilnadu State Dept. of Archaeology, 1978): 16–18, and Vidya Dehejia (1988):101.

3. Jean Filliozat (1972): x–xi.

4. English translations are those of Norman Cutler (1979), P.S. Sundaraṁ (1987), D. Ramaswamy Iyengar (1946) and J.S.M. Hooper (1929), while the French version is by Jean Filliozat (1972).

5. P.S. Sundaram (1987).

6. Dennis Hudson (forthcoming).

7. See Dehejia (1988):180, for stories of Nāyaṉmārs Sirutunaiyar and Kalar–singar.

8. S.A. Tirumalaikorindu Pillai, *Śrīvilliputtūr Sthala Purāṇa*, Madras (1924).

9. While most accounts describe Āṇṭāḷ as an incarnation of Bhūdevī or goddess earth, a variant tradition, frequently heard in modern times, speaks of her as Śrī or Lakṣmī. See Holly Baker Reynolds (forthcoming).

10. Piṉpaḻakiya Jīyar may be dated to the early fourteenth century on the basis of the *Periyatirumuṭi aṭaivu*, which lists him as one of the *śiśyas* or disciples of thirteenth century commentator Periyavāccāṉ Piḷḷai. See S. Krishnaswami Iyengar, ed. (1968): 598.

11. *Periya Tirumoḻi*, 3rd decade, hymn 8, verse 4.

12. For comparative material see Ch. 1 "The Age of a Pious Queen" in V. Dehejia (forthcoming), *The Art of the Imperial Cholas*, New York: Columbia University Press.

13. *South Indian Inscriptions*, Ch. 24 (Madras: Government Press), No. 114.

14. T. N. Subrahmaniam (1953): 145ff. See below Appendix One.

15. The title *Āmukta–māla–da* has the same meaning as the Tamil *Cūṭi–koṭutta–nācciyār*—"She who gave what (the garland) she had worn." The Telegu work remains untranslated.

16. One might mention that a similar awareness is apparent in the hymns of other Āḻvārs too.

17. For a series of essays devoted to a discussion of the *pāvai* vow, see Holly Baker Reynolds, ed. (forthcoming). See also Dennis Hudson (1980).

18. Norman Cutler (1970):6–7. See also Cutler (forthcoming).

19. The cock crows,
the jungle fowl calls,
come all you maidens
whose eyes are deep
as dark lotuses
growing in urns,
come all whose abode
is the good earth
encircled by mountains.
Let us plunge
into the cool waters,
let us praise
the holy feet of Arivaṉ,
let us live in peace
until the end of time.
Fulfill, O song of our vow.

This verse is quoted in the ninth century Jain work on meter, *Yāpparaṅkalamvirutti*, which has an eleventh century commentary, and perhaps predates Āṇṭāḷ. See M. Arunachalam, *Tamiḻ Ilakkiya Varalāṟu. Tamiḻ Pulavar Varalāṟu: 9 Nuṟṟantu* (Tirucirrampalam: Gandhi Vidyalayam, 1969 —):349–351. A later Jain *pāvai* of twenty verses, attributed to the fourteenth century author Avirotinātar, closely follows the format of Māṇikkavācakar's poem. For the text of the later Jain *pāvai*, see S. Kasturi (1971).

20. For a translation of this passage, see Norman Cutler (1979): 9. Also Cutler (forthcoming).

21. For a discussion of this Śaivite *pāvai* song, see Glenn Yocum (forthcoming), and Norman Cutler (forthcoming).

22. See Dennis Hudson (1980) for a perceptive analysis and lucid explication of this theme, drawing upon Periyavāccāṉ Piḷḷai's time–honored commentary.

23. Ibid, 555.

24. Francois Gros and T.V. Gopal Iyer, eds. *Tevaram: Hymnes Sivaites du pays Tamoul. Vol. II. Appar et Cuntarar* (Pondicherry: Institut Francais d'Indologie, 1985), Bk 6, hymn 63:318–19 *ceḻunīrtiraḷai ceṉṟāṭiṉēṉē*. Tiruvānaikkā enshrines an *āpa linga* or linga in the form of waters and so the imagery is, in fact, quite direct.

25. For instance P. Sundaram (1987).

26. Additional meanings given in R. Kasthuri (1971):14, include *karuviḷi* flower, *kurava* flower, ginger root, and a dance.

27. See Appendix Two below for a discussion on this commentator.

28. This is very close to "O our lady" suggested by Dennis Hudson (forthcoming). See also Hudson (1980).

29. See Norman Cutler (1979):n. 32, p. 26.

30. T.P. Meenakshisundaram (1968).

31. Friedhelm Hardy (1983):481–552.

32. Ibid, 449.

33. Cutler points out (private correspondence) that "one could argue that Āṇṭāḷ imagines herself to be a gopī (this is strongly suggested in the *Tiruppāvai*) and she expresses this theme in *Nācciyār Tirumoḻi* in the first person."

34. Friedhelm Hardy (1983):355.

35. Norman Cutler (forthcoming) points out, for example that *Tiruppāvai*, song twenty-three, in which Kṛṣṇa is likened to a mountain lion who has just awoken from his sleep, is modeled on *Puranānūṟu* fifty-two and seventy-eight.

36. A. K. Ramanujan (1967).

37. A. K. Ramanujan (1985):249.

38. Norman Cutler (1988):61–68. See also Cutler (forthcoming) for a discussion of the manner in which Āṇṭāḷ combined in her poetry, elements of both the *akam* (love) and *puṟam* genres of the Caṅkam anthologies.

39. A. K. Ramanujan (1981):160.

40. A. K. Ramanujan (1985):280.

41. See Norman Cutler (forthcoming) for a further discussion of prosody and the importance of the musical tradition. For a comprehensive discussion of this aspect, in a Śaiva context, see Indira Viswanathan Peterson, *Songs to Śiva : The Hymns of the Tamil Saints* (Princeton:Princeton University Press, 1989):76–91.

42. A. K. Ramanujan (1981):161–164.

43. Norman Cutler (1988), especially Ch. 1, "Poet, God and Audience in the Poetry of the Tamil Saints":19–38.

44. Ibid, 27.

45. Ibid, 28.

46. See Cutler (1988): 7, for a sophisticated discussion of this point.

47. A. K. Ramanujan (1973):38.

48. Dennis Hudson (forthcoming).

49. For a brief but penetrating analysis of this theme, see A.K. Ramanujan (1982).

50. Dennis Hudson (forthcoming).

51. Friedhelm Hardy (1983):427.

Tiruppāvai: The Path to Kṛṣṇa

1

On this auspicious day,
full moon in the month of Mārkaḷi,
come beloved young maidens
of blessed Āyarpāṭi,
come adorned with jewels,
come all who wish
to bathe in the limpid waters.

Dark–bodied one,
face fiery as the sun,
soft as the moon,
with eyes like pink lotus;
that young lion,
child of Yaśodā of beauteous eyes,
son of Nandagōpa
ready with the sharp spear,
that Nārāyaṇa himself
will fulfill our desires.

Come join us in this Mārkaḷi vow,
all will applaud you.

Fulfill, O song of our vow.

2

People of the world,
O listen to the rules we observe
for our *pāvai* vow.

Bathing at dawn,
we sing the praises of the supreme one
who slumbers upon the milky ocean.
We eat no ghee, drink no milk,
wear no flowers in our hair,
no kohl in our eyes,
we do no wrong, speak no evil,
we bestow in abundance,

give alms humbly to those who seek,
in this manner
we gladly live.

Fulfill, O song of our vow.

3

We bathe in the clear waters
at the break of dawn.
We sing the glories of the supreme lord
who spanned the worlds
and measured them.
Eternal prosperity surely will be ours.

Our land will be free from evil;
three times a month
there will be abundant rain;
in flooded fields of tall red paddy
carp will jump and play;
spotted beetles will idly dream
in bright blossoms of water lily;
our pots will overflow with milk
from the heavy udders
of our cows,
large, placid, yielding.
Plentiful indeed our gain.

Fulfill, O song of our vow.

4

Beloved god of rain
you dive into the ocean,
scoop and drink its waters,
you rise into the skies—
do not hold back your wealth.

Your form is dark as the hue
of the primordial lord

of the deluge.
Your lightning flashes like
the brilliant discus in the hand
of Padmanābhā
of broad-shouldered beauty.
Your thunder resembles
the resonance of his
Valampurī conch.

Like the stream of arrows
from his *sāranga* bow,
rain upon us, do not delay.
Let plenty come to all
as we joyously dip
in the Mārkaḷi waters.

Fulfill, O song of our vow.

5

O lord of illusion
who dwells on the banks
of the sacred brimming Yamunā,
lord of Maturai of the north,
radiant light of the cowherd clan,
Dāmodara whose birth
brought fame to his mother,
In purity and innocence
we come to worship at your feet
strewing fragrant flowers,
your form held in our minds,
your name upon our tongues.

Chant the names of the lord—
like cotton by fire
all past sins will be consumed,
what future sins may come
will vanish too.

Fulfill, O song of our vow.

6

Young maiden, leave your sleep.
Do you not hear the warble
of the early morning birds?
Or the deep sound
of the silvery conch
calling from the temple of Garuḍa's lord?

The primal cause
slumbers on the serpent
upon the cosmic waters.
He once sucked the poison
from the breast of the demoness.
With a single kick
he shattered the cart
of treacherous Śakaṭa.

The sages and yogis
in whose heart the lord abides
are chanting his holy name.
O maiden, sleep no more.
Arise and join us
for the melodious name of Hari
reverberating
through the air
has entered our souls,
brought us surpassing peace.

Fulfill, O song of our vow.

7

You crazy child,
do you not hear
the noisy chatter of blackbirds
that fills the morning air?
Or the jingle of necklaces
worn by the fragrant–haired
women of Āyarpāṭi?
Do you not hear

the swish of the buttermilk
as the churning rod
moves to and fro?

O noble maiden,
what prompts you to sleep
when we stand here singing
the glories of Nārāyaṇa
who came to us as Keśava?

Bright maid,
arise from your sleep,
open the door.

Fulfill, O song of our vow.

8

Pale dawn lightens the skies.
For a brief while
buffaloes move out
to graze upon the dewy grass.
Barring the way
of maidens going out to bathe,
we brought them here.
We wait, calling out to wake you.
O eager maiden
leave your sleep, join us.

If we honor and serve
the lord who destroyed the Mallas,
split open the mouth of the horse–demon,
if we beseech the supreme being,
leader of the gods,
extol him—
surely his grace
will descend upon us.

Fulfill, O song of our vow.

9

O cousin mine
asleep upon a couch
in a splendid mansion
lit by the glimmer of lamps
where incense fills the air,
leave your slumber,
open your jeweled door.

Aunt, your daughter does not speak.
Is she perhaps dumb
or is she deaf?
Or is she perchance a lazy one?
Has a spell bound her,
kept her captive?
Is she held in a stupor?

We chant the holy names of the lord,
Mādhavan̲, lord of Vaikuṇṭa,
Himself the great illusion—
Aunt, will you not awaken her?

Fulfill, O song of our vow.

10

O fortunate maiden
whose penance
has heaven as its goal,
will you not answer us?
Will you not open the door?

If we worship Nārāyaṇa
whose hair is adorned
with the fragrant holy basil,
that holy one
will grant our desires.

In ancient days
did Kumbhakarṇa lose to you?

Falling into the jaws of death
did he perhaps bequeath to you
his profound slumber?
You slothful one, bright gem,
do not sleep, open the door.

Fulfill, O song of our vow.

11

O golden creeper
of the clan of cowherds,
those innocent ones
who milk young herds of cows,
face their enemies,
strip them of strength.

O peacock of the woods,
with stomach smooth and curved
like the snake's dancing hood,
arise and join
your friends and relatives.

We have entered your porch.
we sing the glories of the
lord dark as the rain cloud.
O fortunate maiden
what avails it to slumber thus
with no movement,
no speech?

Fulfill, O song of our vow.

12

O younger sister
of a plenteous cowherd home,
your lowing buffaloes
call fondly to their calves,
the milk flows freely

from their heavy udders,
making a slush on the floor.

Dew falls upon us
as we cling to the lintel
of your doorway.
We celebrate the fame of the beloved lord
whose righteous anger
destroyed the evil king
of Southern Laṅkā.

Why this senseless slumber
when all around
have arisen?
O speak to us,
now at least awake, join us.

Fulfill, O song of our vow.

13

O maiden whose eyes
put the lotus to shame,
Venus has arisen,
Jupiter has gone to slumber;
bird sounds are ringing
through the morning air.
We extol the glorious deeds
of the lord who split open
the beak of the bird,
cut off the many heads
of wicked Rāvaṇa.

All young maidens
have gathered at the *pāvai* grounds.
Will you alone
refrain from plunging
into the cool waters?
Will you alone lie abed
on this auspicious day?

Give up your pretence,
come maiden, join us.

Fulfill, O song of our vow.

14

In the large pond
of your back garden
pink water lilies unfold,
dark blooms close.
Holy men in ochre robes
with pure white teeth
have walked their unhurried way
to blow the conch,
open the temple doors.

Maiden who promised
to come and wake us,
you are without shame.
Your tongue wags much
but you act not upon your word.
Come let us chant the fame
of the lotus–eyed lord
whose invulnerable hand
holds the discus and conch.

Fulfill, O song of our vow.

15

Young parakeet
are you still asleep?

Stop calling in shrill tones, friends,
I'll be with you soon.

Your words are real clever!
Do we not know of old
your ready tongue?

You indeed are the clever ones!
But never mind—let it be me.

Come, be quick,
what is keeping you?

Has everyone arrived?

They are all here
come count for yourself.

Come sing with us
the prowess of the lord
who killed the vicious elephant,
lord of illusion
whose enemies perish
before his might and valor.

Fulfill, O song of our vow.

16

O watchman
of the portals to the mansion
of our chieftain Nandagōpa,
you who guard
the festooned entrance,
unlock the jeweled door!

The lord of illusion
that dark–hued gem
promised yesterday
to give us the sounding drum.

In purity and innocence
we have come
to awaken him with song.
O friendly sir,
do not refuse our plea,

please open
the tight shut door.

Fulfill, O song of our vow.

17

Awake, O master Nandagōpa,
known for your largesse,
food and drink and clothes
you give to all.

Awake, O mistress Yaśodā,
light of our cowherd clan—
we young stems depend on you,
the open blossom.

O lord of the celestials
whose limitless might
spanned the worlds
and measured them,
leave your sleep, arise.

O Baladeva
adorned with heavy golden anklets,
do not sleep, arise,
your brother and you.

Fulfill, O song of our vow.

18

Daughter–in–law of Nandagōpa
who never shrinks from enemies,
whose strength rivals
an elephant in rut;
O Nappiṉṉāi,
the fragrance of your tresses
fills the air,
please open the door.

The crowing of the cocks
heralds the dawn.
The cooing of flocks of koelbirds
resounds from the bower
of *mātavī* creepers.
O you who hold the ball
between your fingers,
bracelets jingling
upon your lotus hands—
As we chant the names
of your beloved lord,
come joyously, open the door.

Fulfill, O song of our vow.

19

Lord reclining
upon your ivory–legged couch
soft with cotton and silk and down,
lit by the glimmer of tall lamps,
your head upon
the breasts of Nappiṉṉāi
whose hair is braided
with clusters of flowers,
O lord of broad–chested splendor,
speak to us.

You of large kohl–lined eyes,
you do not wish your lord to awaken
however late it be.
You cannot bear to part with him
for even a second.
Is it right to act thus?
Truly, it is not befitting.

Fulfill, O song of our vow.

20

O Redeemer
who appeared before
the thirty–three celestials
and rescued them from fear,
awake, arise.

O lord of great strength
who drives terror
into the hearts of enemies,
spotless lord,
impartial one,
arise from your slumber.

O Nappiṉṉāi of soft rounded breasts,
O lady Śrī,
slender–waisted, coral–lipped,
awaken from your sleep.

Give to us the fan and mirror,
ask your lord
to bathe us right now
in the cooling waters.

Fulfill, O song of our vow.

21

Awake
O son of Nandagōpa,
whose many herds of cows
yield streams of milk
which fill the pots
to overflowing.

O great protector,
supreme lord,
light of lights who came to earth,
awaken from your slumber.

Like those who lose their strength to you,
seek refuge at your door,
bow at your feet,
glorify you in song,
we too have come
to hymn your praises.

Fulfill, O song of our vow.

22

Subduing their pride
the monarchs of the wide earth
crowd beside your couch.
Likewise,
we too gather at your feet.

Will you not glance upon us
with your eyes
opening ever so little
like the slit in the *kinkinī* bell,
like the budding pink lotus?

If you would gaze upon us
with those two beautiful eyes
resembling the sun and moon
rising at once,
indeed,
all our sins will vanish.

Fulfill, O song of our vow.

23

The majestic lion
asleep in his mountain cave
during the season of rains
awakens, opens his fiery eyes,
shakes himself,
his fragrant mane
flying in all directions,

then roars,
stretches his length,
comes forth.

O lord dark as the *pūvai* blossom,
come forth thus
from your seclusion.
Seated upon
your resplendent lion–throne,
consider our request.
Let your grace
be with us.

Fulfill, O song of our vow.

24

Once you measured the worlds—
  glory be to your feet.
You killed the king of Southern Laṅkā—
  glory be to your valor.
You kicked and shattered the cart—
  glory be to your fame.
Like a twig,
you flung and killed the calf—
  glory be to your jeweled anklet.
You held aloft the mountain
as umbrella—
  glory be to your greatness.
You destroy all enmity—
  glory be to the lance in your hand.

In these many ways
do we sing your heroic deeds.
We have come today
to ask for our heart's desire.
Let your grace touch us.

Fulfill, O song of our vow.

25

Born as one woman's son,
that same night you became
the son of another—
in secret you grew in her home.

When in fear and wrath
Kaṃsa made evil plans
seeking to kill you,
you did foil them.
O Neṭumāl,
as fire you were to him.

We come to beseech you.
If you would grant our heart's desires,
we shall ceaselessly sing
your valor, your brilliance,
your glory which befits
the luster of Śrī.
And all our sorrows
will be as yesterday—
forever
shall we rejoice.

Fulfill, O song of our vow.

26

Almighty lord
dark as the sapphire,
if you wish to know our needs
for the Mārkaḷi bath in the waters,
here is what our elders say.

Give us conches
as milky white as your Pāñcacanya
whose sound drives terror
into the hearts of enemies,
large sounding drums,
chanters of hymns of praise,

ornate lamps,
banners and canopies.

Lord who slumbers
upon the banyan leaf,
grant us your grace.

Fulfill, O song of our vow.

27

O Govinda of renown
victorious over enemies,
we sing your virtues,
you fulfill our desires.
All the world
shall marvel at
the gifts we receive—
bracelets, armlets, *tōṭus*,
ear pendants, anklets,
numerous jewels.
We shall drape ourselves
in silk.
We shall eat milk–rice
so covered with ghee
it drips down our elbows.
In joy
together we shall be.

Fulfill, O song of our vow.

28

We humble cowherds
eke out our days
roaming the forests,
grazing our herds.
Little learning ours,
but ours the fortune

that you took birth
in our clan.

O Govinda of excellence
nor you, nor we
may revoke the relationship
between us here.

O supreme lord,
we are artless children.
Forgive us
for hailing you
in familiar ways.
Let your grace be upon us,
grant us our desire.

Fulfill, O song of our vow.

29

At break of dawn
we rise to serve you,
worship at your feet.
Great indeed is our fortune.
Born in our cowherd clan
you cannot deny us,
you are bound to accept
our little services.

O Govinda we have not come
to ask for the ritual drum.
We are your slaves,
we serve only you.
Forever and a day
we shall be connected
with you.
Make all our desires
flow to you alone.

Fulfill, O song of our vow.

30

The cowherd maidens of Āyarpāṭi
adorned with bright jewels,
faces radiant like the moon,
worshipped at the feet of Keśava,
of Mādhava who churned
the ship–laden ocean.
They received from him
their heart's desire.

This tale was told
by Kōtai of the chief of *paṭṭars*
of beautiful Putuvai,
who wore a garland
of cool fresh lotuses.

This reward will be theirs
who chant together
faultlessly
this Tamil garland of thirty songs—
the grace of Tirumāl,
will be upon them—
that lord of limitless wealth,
of holy countenance and lotus eyes,
whose four great shoulders
rise high as hills.
They will live in joy
for ever more.

Fulfill, O song of our vow.

Notes to Tiruppāvai

The first five songs of *Tiruppāvai* are of an introductory nature: they tell us that the aim of the Mārkaḷi *pāvai* vow is to gain from Kṛṣṇa the *parai*, literally the ritual drum (song 1), they give the rules to be observed during the vow (song 2), speak of the prosperity that will ensue for the entire land as a result of such a vow (songs 3, 4), and the benefit to individuals in that all their accumulated sins will disappear (song 5). Having thus set the scene, Āṇṭāḷ devotes the next ten verses awakening maidens to bathe in the cool waters and participate in the joy of being with others who are awake. The girls then gain access to Nandagōpa's house (song 16), awaken the household (song 17), and then rouse Kṛṣṇa's cowherd wife, Nappiṉṉai (songs 18–20), beseeching her aid in reaching Kṛṣṇa. They then awaken Kṛṣṇa himself, praise him and ask him for the *parai*, to be understood as their heart's desire (songs 21–25). They request from him the ritual objects they need to complete the performance of the Mārkaḷi vow (song 26), and receive rich gifts from him to mark the completion of their vow (song 27). The penultimate song may be seen to hold the key to the deeper understanding of *Tiruppāvai*. It reveals that the *parai*, or ritual drum, that the girls have been asking for (songs 1, 8, 16, 24–30), and which we have translated all along as heart's desire (except in songs 26 and 29), has a symbolic meaning. Here the girls tell Kṛṣṇa that they have not come to him for the *parai* (drum); rather, they have come to establish an intimacy with him, a relationship that will endure till the end of time. The last song is a signature verse in which Āṇṭāḷ, identifying herself, confirms that the young maidens did indeed receive the *parai* from Kṛṣṇa, indicating that the lord is pleased and has given them the honor of serving him. It tells us that those who chant her verses in groups will be blessed by Kṛṣṇa and live in joy forever. The *parai* that the girls request from Kṛṣṇa is the symbol of what each aspiring soul wishes to obtain through Kṛṣṇa's grace. It may be the plenty of this world (songs 3, 26, 27), or it may be the service of the divine (songs 28, 29), and the peace and joy obtained thereby. (For a lucid explication of the significance of *Tiruppāvai*, see Dennis Hudson (1980).)

P. 43 line 2 — Mārkaḷi: the Tamil month corresponding to mid–December to mid–January. The months of the Tamil solar calendar occupy fixed positions in the solar year, commencing around the middle of each Western month.

P. 43 line 4 — Āyarpāṭi: cowherd village, Tamil for Gokula or the cowherd village near Vṛindāvan.

P. 43 lines 13, 14 — Nandagōpa and Yaśodā: foster parents of Kṛṣṇa, who was born to Devaki and her husband Vasudeva. Devakī's cousin, the wicked King Kaṃsa, heard a prophecy to the effect that Devakī's eighth child would kill him, and he hence decided to kill each of her children as soon as they were born. At the birth of Kṛṣṇa, the eighth child, Vasudeva secretly carried him to the home of Yaśodā, wife of cowherd Nandagōpa, and exchanged the baby for the infant girl that Yaśodā had just borne. It was thus that Kṛṣṇa, saved from Kaṃsa's plans to kill him, grew up as a cowherd.

P. 43 line 16 — Nārāyaṇa: a name of Viṣṇu in his role as cosmic creator who reclines upon the primeval waters known as *nāra*.

P. 43 line 23 — *pāvai*: the vow in which young girls undertake to bathe at dawn every morning in the month of Mārkaḷi and then praise the lord in order to ensure a happy married life.

P. 43 line 26 One who slumbers on the milky ocean: a reference to Viṣṇu, as cosmic creator, as he reclines upon the serpent Ananta who floats upon the waters of the primeval ocean. The surging, billowing waters are frequently described as "milky."

P. 44 lines 8, 9 Lord who spanned the worlds and measured them: a reference to Viṣṇu's incarnation as *Vāmana*, the dwarf who appeared before the demon King Bali who was once master of the whole world. The dwarf asked for the gift of as much land as he could cover in three strides. Once Bali had poured into his palm the water that ratified the gift, Viṣṇu assumed the gigantic form of Trivikrama. With one stride he covered the earth, with the second stride, the heavens, and turning to Bali he asked where he should place his third stride. Realizing that this was the great Viṣṇu himself, Bali humbly bowed his head and indicated that the lord should place his third stride upon his (Bali's) head. Viṣṇu did so and thus dispatched Bali to the nether world. For details of this story see Wendy O'Flaherty (1975):175–179. Āṇṭāḷ makes frequent allusions to this important story from Viṣṇu legend.

P. 44 line 30
P. 45 line 1 Primordial lord of the deluge: a reference to Viṣṇu's incarnation as the fish, *Matsya*, to save Manu, the ancestor of man, from being destroyed in the universal deluge that swept over the earth. See O'Flaherty (1975):179–184.

P. 45 line 4 Padmanābhā: a name of Viṣṇu; literally "He with the lotus in his navel." The name refers to the creation myth in which a lotus, containing the god Brahmā, grows out of Viṣṇu's navel while he slumbers on his serpent couch that floats on the waters of the cosmic ocean. Brahmā was allotted the task of creating the worlds.

P. 45 line 8 Valampurī: Viṣṇu's sacred conch which has its spirals turning towards the right. The conch with spirals towards the left, the Iṭampurī conch, is the more common variety, used for producing conch shell bangles and the like.

P. 45 line 10 *sāranga*: the name of the bow wielded by Viṣṇu.

P. 45 line 21 Dāmodara: a name of Kṛṣṇa; literally in Sanskrit "One with a rope tied around his belly." The name refers to the time that mother Yaśodā tied young Kṛṣṇa to a mortar for stealing the butter she had just churned.

P. 46 line 6 Garuḍa: Viṣṇu's mount, the divine eagle.

P. 46 lines 10, 11 He once sucked the poison: Pūtanā was a demoness sent by Kaṃsa to destroy Kṛṣṇa. Taking the form of a gracious woman, she searched in Nanda's village until she found the infant and gave him her poisonous breast milk to suck. Kṛṣṇa sucked out her life's breath with her milk and Pūtanā (Stinking One) dropped dead after resuming her ogress form. See O'Flaherty (1975): 214–218.

P. 46 line 14 Śakaṭa: a reference to one of the exploits of baby Kṛṣṇa, in which he killed a demon who had turned himself into a cart (*śakaṭa*), by over–turning the cart with his infant foot.

P. 47 line 8 Keśava: a name given to Kṛṣṇa that refers, probably, to his killing of the winged horse–demon Keśi.

P. 47 line 24 Mallas: a reference to the great wrestling match at Mathurā in which the evil King Kaṃsa pitted his most powerful wrestlers against Kṛṣṇa and Balarāma; the match immediately preceded the killing of Kaṃsa by Kṛṣṇa.

P. 47 line 25 horse–demon: the killing of this winged demon Keśi was one of the exploits of Kṛṣṇa, and probably resulted in his name, Keśava.

P. 48 line 16 Mādhava: name of Kṛṣṇa. The etymology is uncertain, but the name may derive from *madhu* meaning "springtime."

P. 48 line 16 Vaikuṇṭa: the heaven of Viṣṇu.

P. 48 line 27 holy basil: the *tulasī*, a variety of basil sacred to Viṣṇu.

P. 48 line 31 Kumbhakarṇa: brother of the great demon–king Rāvaṇa of Laṅkā, who won a boon from Brahmā, but through a slip of his tongue, acquired the gift of eternal sleep.

P. 50 lines 8, 9 destroyed the king of Southern Laṅkā: a reference to Viṣṇu's incarnation as Rāma,

	and his destruction of demon–king Rāvaṇa of Lȧnkā.
P. 50 lines 18, 19	Venus has arisen/Jupiter has gone to slumber: a concomitance of planets, on the basis of which astronomical calculations have been made for the date of Āṇṭāḷ.
P. 50 lines 23, 24	split open the beak of the bird: a reference to an incident from Kṛṣṇa's boyhood days when a demon took the form of a giant crane (*baka*), pounced upon Kṛṣṇa and imprisoned him in his beak. Unable to bear the burning heat of Kṛṣṇa, the bird–demon Baka threw him up, whereupon Kṛṣṇa took hold of one mandible in each hand, and easily split apart the evil bird.
P. 50 lines 25, 26	cut off the many heads of wicked Rāvaṇa: a reference to the great battle between Rāma and the many–headed demon–king Rāvaṇa, in which, as Rāma felled head after head, a new one grew in its place.
P. 52 line 10	who killed the vicious elephant: The evil King Kaṃsa sent a demon in the form of an elephant, Kuvalayāpīḍa, to trample and kill Kṛṣṇa and his half–brother Balarāma. Kṛṣṇa effortlessly broke its tusks and slew the elephant.
P. 52 line 17	Nandagōpa: Kṛṣṇa's foster father, here pictured as the lord of Āyarpāṭi. The following verses describe his strength and valor, his wealth and generosity.
P. 53 lines 14, 15	who spanned the worlds and measured them: See note to P. 44 lines 8, 9.

P. 53 line 17 Baladeva: son of Nandagōpa and Yaśodā, and hence half–brother (elder) to Kṛṣṇa.

P. 53 line 26 Nappin͟n͟ai: Krsna's cowherd wife, unknown to the tradition of Northern India. Nappin͟n͟ai appears in Tamil legend as early as the *Cilappatikāram*, dated to ca. 450 A.D.; at a much later date (twelfth century onwards) she was considered to be a transcendent being and a form of goddess Nīlādevī.

P. 55 line 1 Kali: We have translated this term as "Redeemer." According to Hindu legend there are four ages: *kṛta, trēta, dvāpara* and the present evil one of *kali*. It is believed that Viṣṇu will appear in this *kali* age, in his tenth incarnation as Kalki, riding upon a flaming horse, to redeem the world from evil.

P. 55 line 3 thirty-three celestials: these gods of one of Indra's heavens, are the eight Vāsus, eleven Rudrās, twelve Ādityās and the two Aṣvini devās.

P. 55 lines 12, 13 O Nappin͟n͟ai/O lady Śrī : Āṇṭāḷ here seems to identify Nappin͟n͟ai with goddess Śrī.

P. 57 line 13 You measured the worlds: See note to P. 44 lines 8, 9.

P. 57 line 15 You killed the king of Southern Lȧnkā: See note to P. 50, lines 8, 9.

P. 57 line 17 You kicked and shattered the cart: See note to P. 46 line 14.

P. 57 lines 19, 20 Like a twig/you flung and killed the calf:

Kṛṣṇa killed a demon named Vatsa who had transformed himself into a calf, by picking him up by the hind leg, and flinging him against a tree, which was another demon in disguise.

P. 57 lines 22, 23 — You held aloft the mountain as umbrella: Kṛṣṇa persuaded the cowherds to worship the mountain Govardhana rather than Indra, god of thunder and rain. In his fury, Indra sent down a torrential rainstorm that threatened to sweep away the inhabitants of Gokula. Quickly Kṛṣṇa lifted up the mountain Govardhana with one hand and held it up as a sheltering umbrella.

P. 58 lines 1–4 — Born as one woman's son. . . .: See note to P. 43 lines 13, 14. Kṛṣṇa was born to Devakī and her husband Vasudeva, but was taken that same night to the cowherd home of Yaśodā and Nandagōpa and exchanged for Yaśodā's new born infant; Kṛṣṇa thus grew up as a cowherd youth.

P. 58 line 6 — Kaṃsa made evil plans: All the demons Kṛṣṇa killed, including the crane–demon, horse–demon, ass–demon and elephant–demon, were part of Kaṃsa's plans to destroy Kṛṣṇa.

P. 59 line 14 — *tōṭus* : ear–studs.

P. 60 lines 9–11 — Forgive us/for hailing you/in familiar ways: One is reminded of Arjuna's words to Kṛṣṇa, in the *Bhagavadgītā*, upon getting the stunning experience of Kṛṣṇa's cosmic form:
Forgive me for having, through love, called

you by familiar names such as Kṛṣṇa, Yādava, friend. In whatever way I may have treated you without respect, while at play, reposing, sitting, at meals, when alone with you, or in company, I implore you, forgive me. (Ch. 11:41,42)

P. 61 lines 5, 6 churned the ship–laden ocean: The reference here is to the great battle between the gods and demons to secure the ambrosia of immortality, and to Viṣṇu's assumption of the form of the tortoise. Diving deep into the depths of the cosmic ocean, he provided the firm base upon which Mount Mandara was placed as the churning stick. Wrapping the divine snake Vāsuki around the mountain, the gods and demons churned the ocean to recover various treasures lost in the great deluge. For details, see O'Flaherty (1975): 270–280.

P. 61 lines 15, 17 Caṅkam Tamil garland: The term *caṅkam* may refer to the Caṅkam age anterior to Āṇṭāḷ, and indicate that she is describing her Tamil verses as being of a particular category of literature. On the other hand, *caṅkam* may be taken in its simplest meaning of "together." In view of the communal nature of the worship described in the *Tiruppāvai*, involving all the young girls of Āyarpāṭi, I have chosen to interpret the phrase as a suggestion that its songs should be sung together, in groups.

Nācciyār Tirumoli:
The Anguish of Separation

The English titles given to individual poems are generally translations of the refrains that occur at the end of each verse; in the absence of a refrain, they reflect Āṇṭāḷ's state of mind. The Tamil titles, given below in parentheses, follow the traditional method of identification and represent the initial phrase of each poem.

1

Unite Me With My Lord, O Kāmadeva
(Tai oru tiṅkaḷ)

Through the month of Tai
I swept the ground before my house,
made sacred mandalas of fine sand.
The month of Māci has begun,
I have adorned the street,
offered worship to your brother and you.
How can I live
without the lord of Vēṅkaṭa?
O formless god,
unite me with
the one who holds the fire-tipped discus. 1

At the silvery break of dawn
I bathed in the stream,
lit a sacred fire of tender twigs.
With fine white sand
I decked the street
and kept my vow to you.
Make an arrow of honey-laden flowers,
write on it the name
of the lord dark as the ocean.
Aim me at my target,
the lord who rent open
the beak of the bird.
Kāmadeva, unite me with my chosen one. 2

Three times a day
I worshipped you
with fragrant blossoms
of white thornapple
and crimson forest flame.
If you break your promise now,
my tortured heart

will abuse you.
Make an arrow of flowers,
write on it the name of Govinda,
aim me at my goal,
the all–knowing lord of Vēṅkaṭa—
Maṉmatha, make me one with that Light. 3

O ancient one,
I wrote your name
upon the wall.
For you I drew the sugarcane bow,
banner with emblem of fish,
attendant maidens,
retinue of horses.
From early childhood
I yearned for
the lord of Dvārka,
adored him alone,
dedicated to him
my budding breasts.
Kāmadeva, unite me to him soon. 4

I dedicated my swelling breasts
to the lord who holds
the conch and flaming discus.
If there is even a whisper
of giving me to a mortal,
I shall not live.
O Maṉmatha,
would you permit a roving jackal
to sniff and eat
the sacrificial food
that brahmins offer
to celestial gods? 5

As the month of Paṅkuṉi dawns
I keep my vow to you,
I wend my way
with worshippers young and handsome
chanting verses in your praise.

My lord is dark as
the rain clouds
the purple *kāyā* blossom
the shining *karuviḷai* flower.
Kāmadeva, make the glowing eyes
in the lotus face of my dark lord
glance with grace upon me. 6

I invoke you
with offerings of sugarcane and jaggery,
fresh paddy and flattened rice.
I bow to you,
brahmins chant mantras in your praise.
Maṉmatha,
if you make
Trivikrama who spanned the worlds
caress me with his sacred hands,
my shapely breasts, my slender waist
will bring me fame on earth,
glory eternal. 7

To keep my vow
I eat but once a day,
body neglected, unadorned,
tangled hair in disarray,
lips pale and dry.
O Kāmadeva of eternal glory
for one thing I plead with you,
fulfill my womanhood!
Let glory be mine
that I held the feet of Keśava. 8

Three times a day
I invoke you in prayer,
strewing flowers at your feet.
Maṉmatha,
if I may not serve
the faultless lord
dark as the deep ocean,
my endless tears and piteous cries

will leave their mark upon you.
I shall be like the forlorn bull,
beaten with its own yoke,
driven away
unfed. 9

Bowing to the jeweled feet of Kāmadeva
of the sugarcane bow
and arrows of flowers,
Kōtai of Viṣṇucittaṉ,
master of the people of Putuvai
of storied mansions and hilly tracts,
pleads with Kāmadeva
to unite her with her deep blue lord
who answered the cries of Gajendra,
broke the elephant's tusk,
rent open the beak of the bird.
Those who repeat
this garland of sweet Tamil verses
will attain the feet
of the lord of the celestials.

2

Do Not Break Our Sandcastles (Nāmam āyiram)

Lord praised by a thousand names,
O Nara, O Nārāyaṇa,
you took birth as Yaśodā's son—
we cannot escape your pranks.
The month of Paṅkuṉi is here
we have adorned the street for Kāmadeva,
O naughty Śrīdhara,
do not break
our sandcastles.

With aching backs
we spent the day
building sandcastles.
We had not time
to sit and gaze at them.
Eternal lord,
do not dampen our desire.
Long ago as an infant
you slept on the cosmic ocean
upon the banyan leaf.
That you do not pity us
is our misfortune.

Fierce lion whose resting place
is the cosmic ocean,
you saved Gajendra
from great woe,
do not make our hearts ache
with your sidelong glance,
do not tease us.
With bangle–laden hands
we toiled
sifting sand and silt

to make our playhouses.
You who slumber
upon the surging ocean,
do not break our sandcastles. 3

You dark as the rain clouds,
your charming ways
and sweet words
enchant us,
bind us like a spell.
In truth your face
is a magic mantra.
We are but urchins,
we shall not retort and hurt you,
You of the lotus eyes,
do not break our sandcastles. 4

With soft white sand
we built castles of our fancy.
Along the street we drew
auspicious diagrams—
Keśava, O wicked Mādhava,
have you no eyes to see?
If you erase them
still our hearts will melt
with love for you,
we shall bear you no grudge. 5

We are young children
with budding breasts—
Making our sandcastles your excuse,
you tease and beguile us.
Your words have some meaning
which we do not understand.
Victorious lord
who crossed the ocean,
killed clans of demons,
razed Laṅkā to the ground,
do not torment us. 6

If you spoke such words
to learned men
they would surely understand.
To us ignorant children
they are of no use.
Lord dark as the ocean
we plead in the name of your consorts—
you built the bridge to Laṅkā
do not break our sandcastles. 7

We work happily
with pots and pans
and winnowing tray
to build our sandcastles.
You kick and touch
and break them.
What use to you
such teasing?
Lord dark as the ocean,
holding the flaming discus,
you know well
even jaggery tastes bitter
when in sorrow. 8

You appear
in the center of the courtyard,
you mock and smile,
you break our sandcastles,
you also shatter our hopes.
Govinda
who once spanned the earth,
stretched across the skies
and measured the worlds,
if you stop us here,
put your arms around us,
what will people say? 9

Kōtai of Viṣṇucittan̲, chief of Villiputtūr,
home of those learned in the Vedas
sang these verses

telling of little *gopī* girls
playing in the street,
prattling and beseeching the lord
who tasted the nectar of Sītā's lips
not to destroy their castles of sand.
Those who sing these Tamil verses
will surely reach Vaikuṇṭa. 10

3

Give Back Our Clothes
(Kōli alaippatan munnam)

At break of dawn,
long before the cock crows,
we came to bathe
in the waters of this pond.
The sun has arisen,
we are deeply
humiliated.
Lord who slumbers on the serpent,
my friends and I
raise a hand to beseech you,
we promise
never to return to these waters—
give us back our clothes. 1

O Māl with honeyed basil
knotted in your hair,
alas, what brought you to this pond?
What path did you take?
Lord of illusion, our beloved,
that is not in our destiny.
You wicked boy,
that we will not do.
You who leaped and danced
upon the serpent's head,
return our clothes
from up the wild lime tree. 2

You there,
what is this youthful prank?
If our mothers hear
they would scarce
put up with it.
You upon the flowering lime,

this outrage
you do not recognize.
O lord whose bow destroyed Laṅkā,
we will give you whatever you want,
we will go unseen,
please return our clothes. 3

Looking all around
we plunged to bathe
in the waters of this pond
where many come for a dip.
Little do you see
that we cannot stop
the helpless tears
brimming over.
You who destroyed Laṅkā,
have you no mercy at all?
You king of monkeys,
climber of the wild lime tree,
give us back our clothes. 4

The cutlass fish and the carp
bite our legs—
we are in a pitiful state.
If our elder brothers
come with spears to fight you
do you think it would be fun?
Stop climbing up
the wild lime tree
holding our fine garments.
Handsome dark lord
give us back our clothes. 5

The prickly stem of the lotus
stings our legs
like scorpion poison,
great is our pain.
As for you, O lord,
you play with our water pots
throwing them up and dancing!

Stop your vexing play,
give us back our clothes. 6

We are tired of standing in the waters.
Your game is unfair
the village is too far off.
We are bound to you alone,
but if our mothers see us now
they would indeed be cross.
Lord who alone exists
at the deluge,
do not keep climbing
the flowering wild lime,
throw down our clothes. 7

We are not all from *māmī*'s house—
others too are gathered here.
You of the pure, lotus eyes
who slumbers all night without care,
we tell you in clear terms
no good will come
of this wicked play.
Handsome scion
of the cowherd clan
atop the wild lime tree,
throw down our clothes. 8

Kaṃsa spread his net,
you escaped at dead of night—
was it only to bring grief
to us naked maidens?
Mother Yaśodā spoils you,
lets you have your way.
You who sucked the milk
of the deceitful ghoul,
O shameless one,
give us back our clothes. 9

Kōtai of Viṣṇucittan̲,
chief of the people of Putuvai

of many storeyed houses,
has sung this garland of ten verses
on the mischief that Nampi the dark lord
played upon the *gopīs*.
Those who repeat these verses
will reach Vaikuṇṭa
and abide at the feet
of lord Mādhava. 10

4

Join Up, O *Kūṭal* (Teḷḷiyār palar)

Bounteous lord
whom the gods worship,
bridegroom of Māliruñcōlai—
if I may approach his couch
touch and soothe his holy feet
then join up, O *kūṭal*. 1

He lives in wooded Vēṅkaṭa,
he came to earth as dwarf,
lived in joy, without care.
That lord of Kaṇṇapuram,
if he will hasten to take my hand,
fold me in embrace
then unite, O *kūṭal*. 2

Esteemed lord
praised by Brahmā and the gods,
son of virtuous Vasudeva
and Devakī of the bright forehead,
it that prince will come to me
then join up, O *kūṭal*. 3

They trembled
the *gopīs* and *gopas*.
He climbed upon
the flowering blue *katampa* oak,
he dived into the waters,
danced on captive Kāliya.
If that dancer will but come
then unite, O *kūṭal*. 4

He came in search of Maturai
of palaces and mansions,

walked right into my street.
With a kick
he killed the wild elephant.
If he will come to unite with me
then join, O *kūṭal*. 5

Absolute lord of freedom,
his toddling walk
split the *maruta* trees.
He put an end to Kaṃsa's cunning.
That king of splendid Maturai,
if he will come to me
then join, O *kūṭal*. 6

Once the lord
ended Śiśupāla's unjust acts,
uprooted the *maruta* trees,
killed the seven bulls,
the great bird,
and powerful Kaṃsa
of conquering fame.
If that victor will come to me
then join, O *kūṭal*. 7

He dwells only in the hearts
of those who yearn for him.
Cowherd chief
who plays with calves,
king of Dvārka of fragrant groves,
if he will come to me
then unite, O *kūṭal*. 8

Long ago
in the guise of a brahmin dwarf
he came to Mahābali's great sacrifice,
he spanned the sky and earth
in two giant strides.
If that lord will come to me
then unite, O *kūṭal*. 9

He is the essence
of the ageless Vedas,
he saved the tortured elephant.
Our handsome one
abides in the hearts
of the charming *gopīs*.
If he will come to me
join up, O *kūṭal*. 10

Long–haired Kōtai sang this song
about the cowherd maidens
ever sulking and making up
quarreling and uniting
and of the *kūṭal* game they played.
Those who sing these ten verses
will be free of all sin. 11

5

Koelbird, Call Him To Me
(Maṉṉu perum pukaḻ Mādhavaṉ)

Pining for
Mādhava of eternal fame
dark as the blue sapphire,
crowned with a cluster of gems,
is it right
that the conch shell bangles
should slip off my wrists?
Koelbird who lives in flowery groves
of laurel, pear, wild poppy and *ñāḻal*,
fly to my lord of the coral lips
stay with him,
call his names repeatedly,
ask him
to hasten to my side. 1

The immaculate lord
whose left hand holds
the silvery white conch
shows not his form to me.
He enters my soul,
makes it melt,
plays upon my heart,
tortures me.
Warbling koelbird
drunk with honey
dripping from magnolia flowers,
speak to my lord of Vēṅkaṭa
murmer softly to him,
ask him to come to me. 2

With Mātali as charioteer
he fought demonic Rāvaṇa,
with a stream of arrows

felled his many heads—
Nowhere do I see his form.
O koelbird living with your beloved mate
in groves laden with the fragrance
of fresh–blown flowers,
where humming bees sing,
call my dark gem to me. 3

My bones melt,
my beautiful lance–like eyes
have known no sleep
for many nights.
Sunk in the sea of sorrow,
I whirl round and round—
I do not see
the boat named Vaikuṇṭa.
O koel, you know well
the pangs of parting
from the beloved.
Go to the lord whose emblem
is golden–hued Garuḍa,
ask that holy one
to come to me. 4

I long to gaze
upon the golden feet
of the lord of Villiputtūr
where swans move on the waters.
My eyes, like fighting carps,
have known no rest.
O koel, I will give you
as companion my pet parrot
whom I have fed
on milk and sweetened rice,
if you will but call to the lord
who spanned the worlds,
make him come to me. 5

Hṛṣikeśa
whom all the gods extol
has enslaved me.

I pine, I languish,
I waste away,
losing beauty of breasts,
pink lips and pearly white teeth.
Young koelbird
who sleeps in hilly groves
where flowers grow in clusters,
ask my true one to come to me
and I shall bow to you
in gratitude. 6

So great is my desire
to unite with the lord
who rests upon the milky ocean
that emotion chokes my breath,
by breasts rise and fall
and quiver in joy.
O dainty koel,
what do you gain
by hiding from me?
If you will go
to him who holds
conch, discus and mace,
ask him to come to me,
great indeed will be your merit. 7

Lord of harmony
whose strong arms
wield the *sāranga* bow—
between us we took a vow
known to none other.
Little koelbird
who lives in mango groves
tastes the sweet ripe fruit,
if you will go to Tirumāl
ask him to hasten to me,
you shall see
what I shall do to him. 8

I am caught
in the net of Śrīdhara,

the green–hued lord.
O koel who dwells in groves
where honey bees hum,
listen with care—
Ask him who holds conch and discus
to come to me,
or bring me his golden armlet—
If you wish
to live in this grove,
one of these
you must do for me. 9

I yearn for him
who once measured the worlds.
He has me in his thrall,
I cannot resist his power.
I know not how
the moon and the southern breeze
add to my heartache.
O koel,
do not linger in this grove
and add to my anguish,
go bring Nārāyaṇa to me
else I shall drive you away. 10

Yearning for the lord
dark as the ocean,
this song of the long–eyed maiden
who sent the black koelbird
to beseech the lord
whose long strides measured the worlds
to unite with her,
was sung by Kōtai of Viṣṇucittaṉ,
brahmin chief of Putuvai
where the four Vedas are chanted.
Those who recite
this skillful garland of verses
will forever chant
the name of Nārāyaṇa. 11

6

I Dreamt This Dream, My Friend
(Vāraṇam āyiram)

A thousand elephants followed
as Nāraṇa Nampi walked in state.
The town was adorned
with flags and banners,
at every threshold
stood a blessed golden urn—
I dreamt this dream, my friend. 1

Tomorrow, auspicious day,
the wedding will take place.
A great green awning stood
adorned with shoots of palm and areca.
Entered Mādhava of leonine power
the ox–like youth, Govinda—
I dreamt this dream, my friend. 2

Indra and hosts of gods arrived,
they blest me,
chose me as bride.
The wedding garb
Durgā draped upon me,
she decked me
with bridal garland—
I dreamt this dream, my friend. 3

Waters from the sacred rivers
were sprinkled upon us,
brahmins and *siddhas*
chanted blessings and praise.
The holy one stood adorned
with garlands of pure flowers.
Around our wrists

was tied the sacred yellow thread—
I dreamt this dream, my friend. 4

Young maidens came
to welcome him,
holding golden urns,
lamps glowing like the morning sun.
The lord of Maturai entered
sandal clad,
the earth trembled
to his footsteps—
I dreamt this dream, my friend. 5

The drums beat
the conch shells sounded.
Beneath the awning
festooned with pearls,
Madhusūdana, beloved Nampi
came and took my hand—
I dreamt this dream, my friend. 6

Learned brahmins
chanted Vedic mantras,
placed green *darbha* grass
around the sacrificial fire
lit with twigs.
The lord of great prowess,
strong as a raging elephant,
took my hand,
we walked around the fire—
I dreamt this dream, my friend. 7

Today and in endless future births
Nampi, our lord Nārāyaṇa
will be my constant companion.
With his holy lotus-hands
he placed my foot
upon the *ammī* stone—
I dreamt this dream, my friend. 8

Came my handsome brothers
eyebrows arched like bows,
they drew me forward,
before the fire
they placed my hand
upon the hand of Acutaṉ
of leonine grandeur.
Handfuls of flattened rice
they heaped into the flames—
I dreamt this dream, my friend. 9

They smeared us
with cool saffron
and sandal paste.
We rode upon the elephant,
circling water-sprinkled streets.
They showered upon us
streams of saffron-fragrant water—
I dreamt this dream, my friend. 10

Kōtai of the king of Villiputtūr
town of famed Vaiṣṇavas,
dreamt this dream of the cowherd lord
that she became his.
Those who recite
this pure garland of ten Tamil verses
will live in joy
and bear fine and noble children. 11

7

White Conch From The Fathomless Sea
(Karuppūram nāṟumō)

Do they smell of camphor
or of the lotus bloom?
Do they taste sweet
his sacred lips of coral hue?
O white conch
from the fathomless sea,
I long to know,
tell me the taste,
the fragrance
of the lips of Mādhavaṉ
who broke the elephant's tusk. 1

O fine conch
born in the ocean,
you grew in the body
of the demon Pañcacaṉa.
Now at the sound of your voice
demons tremble with fear,
for you have climbed
into the hand of
the lord of the deluge
and made it your home. 2

O beautiful great conch,
like the full moon
riding the hilltops at midnight
during the season of rains,
you rest in beauty,
forever you dwell
upon the sacred hand of Vāsudeva
lord of Maturai of the north. 3

Indra dare not compete with you
O Valampurī conch.
Shining like the full moon
you rest upon the hand of Dāmodara,
so close to him you are
seeming to whisper
mantras
into his ears. 4

Unknown, forgotten, nameless
are others whose home was the ocean.
You alone, O Pāñcacanya
savor every day
the nectar of the lips
of the great lord
Madhusūdana. 5

O Valampurī
you went not
in search of holy waters—
you climbed into the hand of the lord,
the holiest of *tīrthas*—
you plunge, you revel
in the nectar of the lips
of lotus–eyed Māl
who dragged and broke
the twin *maruta* trees. 6

O, king of conches,
as the swan imbibes
the honey of the fresh pink lotus,
you climbed
into the beauteous hand of Vāsudeva,
dark lord of glowing eyes,
you imbibe
the nectar of his lips.
Great indeed is your glory. 7

Your food,
the nectar of the lips

of the lord who measured the worlds.
Your couch,
the palm of the hand
of the lord dark as the ocean.
O Pāñcacanya
your ways are selfish, unjust.
No wonder women clamor,
quarrel with you. 8

Sixteen thousand *devīs*
cast their envious glances,
like wine, you sip
the nectar of Mādhavaṉ's lips.
If you enjoy alone
what all would share,
will they not complain
O glorious great conch? 9

Kōtai of Viṣṇucittaṉ
famed chief of *paṭṭars*
of beauteous Putuvai
sang this song of Pāñcacanya's
intimacy with lord Padmanābhā.
Those who learn and repeat
these ten Tamil verses
will ever be close to the lord. 10

8

O Dark Rain Clouds
(Viṇ nīla mēlāppu)

O clouds that form a vast canopy,
did my Tirumāl
come with you?
that lord from Vēṇkaṭa
where clear streams flow?
The tears spill
between my breasts
like waterfalls,
saddening me,
consuming my womanhood.
Will this bring him honor? 1

O great clouds
showering raindrops
like golden beads
priceless pearls,
has the dark–hued one of Vēṇkaṭa
that strong lord
sent a message through you?
Tortured by the fire of love,
sleepless at midnight
I toss on my soft couch,
a target for the southern breeze. 2

The glow of youth and color,
the bangles on my hand,
sleep and peace of mind,
all have gone
leaving me empty.
O kind and compassionate clouds,
forlorn I sing the praises of Govinda
who dwells in Vēṅkaṭa
of cool waterfalls—
can that keep me alive? 3

O clouds
from whose body
lightening springs,
tell the lord of Vēṅkaṭa
upon whose glorious body
rests the goddess Śrī,
that I yearn incessantly
that he should desire
the budding breasts
of my radiant body—
that he should come
and fold me in embrace 4

O great rain clouds
that rend the sky,
let your heavy showers
make the honeyed blossoms of Vēṅkaṭa
fall and scatter.
Go to the lord who killed Hiraṇya,
rent him open
with his sharp claws—
tell him to return
the bracelets
he took from me. 5

O cool clouds
that rise into the skies
laden with water,
spread yourselves,
let your showers
fall upon Vēṅkaṭa,
the hill of the lord
who took the earth from Mahābali.
The gnat
entering the woodapple
hollows it—
the lord entering me
has taken all
consumed my womanhood.
O great rain clouds

tell Nāraṇa
of my grievous
love–sickness. 6

O cool clouds,
fall at the sacred feet
of the lotus–eyed lord of Vēṅkaṭa
who churned the conch–laden ocean.
Make this plea—
tell him I will survive
only if he will stay with me
for one day,
enter me
so as to wipe away
the saffron paste
adorning my breasts. 7

O dark clouds
of the dark season of rains,
repeat the names
of the great lord of victory,
the hero of the battlefield
who dwells in Vēṅkaṭa.
Will he not bless me,
one day soon
send word to me?
Else I shall wither and fall
like the lovely *erukku* leaf
in the dry season of summer. 8

O rain clouds
rearing like dark elephants
above the hill of Vēṅkaṭa,
the word of the lord
who slumbers upon the serpent
has turned false.
Forgetting that he is
my sole refuge,
he tortures
this young maiden.

If the world hears of it,
will they speak well of him? 9

From deep longing
for the lord
whose couch is the serpent,
she of the fine forehead
sang of how she sent the rain clouds
as messengers
to place her plea
before the lord of Vēṅkaṭa.
Those who mindfully repeat these Tamil verses
sung by Kōtai of the master of Putuvai
who lacks nothing,
will be bound to the lord forever. 10

9

In The Grove Of My Lord
(Cintura cempoṭi)

The velvety red
of the ladybirds
whose flutter fills the air
in the dark grove of Māliruñcōlai
brings to mind
the glowing red
of the *kumkum* powder
on my dark lorḍ's forehead.
Once he churned the ocean
for the nectar of the gods
using Mandara mountain
as churning rod.
I flounder in the net
of that lord
of the handsome shoulders.
Can I escape
alive? 1

In the flowery grove
of Māliruñcōlai
where young elephants
fight in play,
creepers of white jasmine
remind me of his smile—
clusters of dark mangrove blossoms
laugh mockingly—
I cannot bear it.
O friend,
to whom shall I complain
of the clamor
his garland awakes in my heart? 2

O dark *karuviḷai* blossoms,
purple *kāyā* flowers,
your color brings to mind
the rich glow
of Tirumāl's form—
you have not told me
a way
by which I may survive.
Nampi of Māliruñcōlai,
upon whose broad shoulders
sports the goddess Śrī—
is it right that he enter my home,
wrest the bangles from my hand? 3

You five great sinners,
dwellers in this lush grove
of Māliruñcōlai—
koelbirds, peacocks,
deep blue *karuviḷai* blossoms,
fresh black bilberries,
purple *kāyā* flowers—
what avails you
the dark color
of my lord? 4

O dark rippling ponds,
O pink water lotuses,
O swarms of bees
clinging to the lotus buds—
you who dwell in Māliruñcōlai
where tall flowering groves abound,
you remind me of
my lotus-eyed lord of Vēṅkaṭa
whose dark form glows
like the rain clouds—
O show me a place of refuge. 5

A hundred pots
filled with butter,
a hundred vessels

full of sweetened rice
I have consecrated to Nampi
of the fragrant grove
of Māliruñcōlai.
Will indeed the holy one
come today,
accept these offerings? 6

If he will come
taste my offerings,
I shall consecrate
a hundred thousand more.
Lord of Māliruñcōlai
where the fragrance
of the southern breeze
fills the air—
If, within my heart,
he will unite with me,
I will be his slave
forever more. 7

At dawn
hosts of black warbling sparrows
seem to sing the song
of the coming of Tirumāl—
Can they be right?
My lord of Dvārka,
lord of the mountain grove,
lord who slept upon the banyan leaf—
the sparrows keep repeating
his sacred names. 8

In the hilly grove of Māliruñcōlai
where the glorious buttercup blooms,
I live unprofitable days
hanging in vain
like golden garlands of cassia.
Will ever I hear
the sound of the conch

blown by the sacred lips of my lord,
or the sweet echo of his *sāranga* bow? 9

Kōtai of the curly black tresses
sang this garland of verses
about the handsome lord of Māliruñcōlai
where the Silampu river
dashes against its banks
floating logs of eagle–wood
and fragrant sandal.
Those who sing these ten Tamil verses
will attain
the feet of the lord. 10

10

Thirsting For The Lord
(Kārkōṭal pūkkāḷ)

O dark mangrove flowers,
where is my lord
dark as the ocean
who sent you in battle array
to battle with me?
To whom indeed shall I complain?
My mind runs
hither and thither
seeking his beautiful garland
of sacred basil,
alas! I cannot control it. 1

O flowers gazing upwards,
go above to the celestial worlds,
to that white radiance,
the source of the Vedas,
from whose right hand
arises the glowing discus—
Without its fiery flame
hurting me,
can you gather me
into that region of light
where dwell his saints? 2

O lady *kōvai* vine
do not torment me
with your coral fruit—
I shrink from
the lord of coral lips.
To me who has lost all shame,
the lord whose couch is the serpent,
is double–tongued
like his own serpent,
unfortunate one that I am. 3

O lady jasmine,
torment me not with your smiles.
O graceful creeper,
I take refuge in you.
If the word of him
whose brother cut the nose
of the evil ghoul
should prove to be false,
my very birth is a falsehood. 4

O singing koelbirds
what song is this?
If the lord of Vēṅkaṭa
shows me a way to live,
come and sing.
If the lord
of the flying Garuḍa banner
bestows his grace upon me,
if he unites with me,
then may you sing,
then shall I listen. 5

O grand hosts of peacocks
with stately walk
and practiced dance,
I fall at your feet.
Your color and form
remind me of lord Kaṇṇaṉ.
O, see the piteous state
in which he has left me,
that self–same beloved
who from time immemorial
reclines upon
the dancing, hooded serpent. 6

O handsome peacocks
who dance
with outspread plumes,
alas, unfortunate one,
I have not eyes to watch

your dance.
That chieftain, Govinda,
dancer with the waterpots
tortures me.
He has tricked me, taken all,
made me his slave.
Not any more
can you torment me. 7

O rain clouds
seeming like dark clay outside,
liquid wax within,
rain down upon Vēṅkaṭam
where the handsome lord dwells.
Help me to find within me
my beloved.
When he folds me
in close embrace
melts my heart,
then rain down upon us. 8

O great deep ocean,
the lord entered into you,
mixed and churned you,
deprived you of your nectar.
That lord of illusion
entered into me too,
churned me,
drained me of my essence.
Go to the serpent
who is the lord's couch,
tell him of my endless sorrow
that he may plead for me. 9

My dear friend,
what can we mere mortals do
about our great glorious lord,
the omnipotent one
who slumbers upon the serpent?
If Viṣṇucittaṉ of Villiputuvai

invokes his lord in his special way,
if the lord reveals himself,
then we too may see him.

11

He Has Taken All
(Tām uhakkum)

O friends
adorned with jewels,
are not the conch–shell bangles
on my hands
as dear to me
as the conch he loves
which rests upon his hand?
Lord of sacred Araṅkam
stretched upon
the fire–tongued serpent,
alas, my friends
he does not even
glance at me! 1

O lovely ladies,
my honeyed lord of Araṅkam
of beauteous hair
beauteous lips
beauteous eyes,
that beauteous lord
from whose navel
the lotus emerges,
whose beauty is beyond compare,
he who is mine
has loosened my bracelets
forever. 2

Sovereign lord
who faultlessly rules
the heavenly spheres,
the earth
encircled by billowing seas—
my lord of splendor

of scepter and crown
who reigns in holy Araṅkam—
surely my bangles
can add naught
to his perfection! 3

Lord of Araṅkam
of stately walls and storeyed mansions,
immaculate lord
who as dwarf
in days gone by
begged for alms—
as if that were not enough,
he set his heart upon my bangles.
Then, will he not
walk by this street? 4

My lord of cool Araṅkam
where live men of virtue,
he whose couch is the serpent—
long ago
in the deceptive form
of dwarf
he received in his hands
the gift-giving waters,
took possession
of all the worlds.
If now he takes
the little wealth of my hands,
he takes
that which naught enriches him. 5

Already
his hands have taken
the wealth of my hands—
lord of holy Araṅkam
where Kavēri waters
flood the paddy fields.
Present everywhere,
yet unapproachable,

that lord who is the
essence of the four Vedas
has caught the essence
of my body. 6

He neither ate nor slept—
bound by desire for the beloved,
torn by the pangs of separation,
he rent apart the roaring ocean.
That sovereign lord
of strong–walled Araṅkam
remembers not the suffering,
remembers the good alone. 7

Once long ago
for the sake of the maiden earth
forlorn in moss–ridden body,
he took the shameful form
of a filthy
water–dripping boar.
That radiant one
famed lord of holy Araṅkam—
the words that he spoke to me
can never be erased
from my mind. 8

All was set for the wedding—
Śiśupāla was resolved
to take her hand in marriage.
All of a sudden
his glow vanished,
he stood petrified.
The divine bridegroom
stepped in,
took her hand in marriage.
Araṅkam
is the name of his
chosen abode. 9

"I shall love and uplift
those who love and adore me"—
Viṣṇucittaṉ has heard
these great and noble words
spoken by
the lord of Araṅkam.
If the lord
who is truth
does not uphold his word,
who indeed can affirm it?

12

Take Me To The Land Of My Lord
(Maṟṟu iruntīr)

None of you understand
how I fret and pine
for the love that is Mādhavaṉ.
The words you utter
are like the deaf
speaking to the dumb.
Leaving the mother who bore him,
Nampi grew
in the home of another.
He faced the warring Mallas
in Maturai—
please take me
to that holy city. 1

Of what avail to cling to shame?
Now all the neighbors know.
If you would see me
as once I used to be,
there rests but one cure.
If I set eyes on
that lord of illusion
who came as dwarf
to measure the worlds,
I shall be well.
If you wish to save me
then do not delay,
decree
that I be taken to Āyarpāṭi. 2

If word gets around
I left my parents
home and family,
went my lonesome way,

it will be too late
to save my name.
The lord of illusion
has shown his form to me,
that son of Nandagōpa
who incites quarrels,
lays the blame
upon others.
To the threshold
of Nandagōpa's house,
take me at dead of night. 3

They will behold
the face of none but
the lord who holds the discus
in his lustrous palm.
These breasts of mine
clad in red *choli*
close their eyes,
draw back in shame
from mere mortals.
They will not go
to any but Govinda.
No longer can I live here—
take me please
to the banks of the Yamunā. 4

Dear mothers
grieve not for me,
none may understand my sickness.
There is one, dark as the ocean—
if his hand
should stroke me,
I shall be whole again.
He climbed
the *katampa* oak
that stood along
the river bank,
he leaped upon Kāliya's head,
danced a furious dance.

To that battlefield
along those holy waters,
O take me please. 5

Cool rain clouds,
karuviḷai blossoms,
kāyā flowers, lotuses,
again and again they urge me
to go to Hṛṣikeśa.
Tired, sweating, hungry,
knowing that the time had come
to get his share
of sacrificial food,
he watched,
he waited long.
To that Bhaktavilōcana
O, take me soon. 6

My color has changed,
my mind has weakened,
I have lost
all shame,
my lips are pale,
I have not taken
a morsel of food,
my very soul
is listless.
There be one
dark as the ocean,
if they place around my neck
his garland of sacred basil
cool and green,
then alone shall I revive.
To that banyan tree at Bāndiram
where Balarāma fought Pralamba
O take me, please. 7

He tended calves
you call him cowherd!
He wandered the forests

you call him peasant!
He was bound to the mortar,
you sinners, you deride him!
Is all this fun for you?
Do not repeat
what you have heard,
else I shall abuse you.
Holding in victory
the mountain as umbrella
he saved
from pouring rain
the herds of cows.
Take me to that Govardhana
of hallowed fame. 8

"Govinda! Govinda!"
my parrot calls from its cage.
If I scold it, refuse it food,
it calls out loudly
"O lord who measured the worlds!"
Friends, do not lose your fair name
do not earn dishonor.
Send me soon
to that city of stately mansions—
take me to Dvārka. 9

Deeply determined
to reach the land of her lord,
beginning with famed Maturai,
ending with Dvārka,
glossy-haired Kōtai of Viṣṇucittaṉ,
chief of Putuvai
of dazzling mansions,
made the daring plea
that her people take her
to his dwelling place.
Vaikuṇṭa is the abode
of those who sing
this garland of fine verses. 10

13

The Agony Of Desire
(Kaṇṇaṉ eṉṉum)

I hunger and thirst
for a sight
of Kaṇṇaṉ, my dark lord.
Don't stand aside
mocking me—
your words sting
like sour juice
poured upon an open wound.
Go bring the yellow silk
wrapped around the waist
of him who knows not
the sorrow of women—
fan me with it,
cool the burning of my heart. 1

I am caught in the snare
of that omniscient lord
who slumbered
upon the banyan leaf.
Do not speak
whatever comes to mind—
your words pierce me
like a dagger.
The cowherd chief
who tends his calves
with staff in hand,
that dancer with the waterpots
who reclines in sacred Kuṭantai—
bring me
his sacred basil
cool, lustrous, blue,
place it
upon my soft tresses. 2

Like an arrow
from the bow of his eyebrows,
the sidelong glance
of him who destroyed Kaṃsa
enters my heart,
makes me sore with pain,
weak and worn.
I yearn, I melt,
yet he says not
"have no fear."
If willingly
he gives his garland
of holy basil,
bring it,
place it upon my breast. 3

Who can offer me solace?
That black bull
who stole the hearts
of all in Āyarpāṭi
has trampled upon my heart,
broken and crushed it.
Go to the lord,
himself the nectar
that never cloys,
bring me the nectar
from his hallowed mouth,
sprinkle it upon me,
wipe away my pain. 4

I weep
I sing his glories—
he shows not his form.
He says not
"have no fear."
He does not come close,
nor caress, nor embrace me,
he does not pervade me.
Through the leafy glades
where his cows graze

comes the sound of the flute
that Neṭumāl plays.
Bring me the cool nectar
from the mouth of his flute,
spread it upon my face
it will revive me. 5

In this ignoble world
where he roamed
as son of Nandagōpa,
selfish, cruel Tirumāl
has tortured me.
I am bound
to the spot
where he placed his feet—
I am powerless
to move.
Bring me the dust
from the footprints
left by that insensitive lord—
smear it upon my body
that life may linger. 6

He who flies
the victory banner of Garuḍa,
whom all the worlds exalt,
his mother reared him
like the bitter margosa tree
to serve no purpose.
To wipe away the sorrow
of these innocent breasts,
the sorrow of not finding him,
hold them tight
against his youthful shoulders,
bind them there. 7

My soul melts in anguish—
he cares not
if I live or die.
If I see the lord of Govardhana

that looting thief,
that plunderer,
I shall pluck
by their roots
these useless breasts,
I shall fling them
at his chest,
I shall cool
the raging fire
within me. 8

To soothe the grief
of my rounded breasts,
is it not better
in this very birth
to serve Govinda
in little intimate ways,
than wait for a life beyond?
If one day
he would fold me
into his radiant chest,
that would fulfill me.
Else, looking straight at me,
uttering the truth,
he should give me
leave to go—
that also would I accept. 9

Kōtai of Viṣṇucittan̲
master of the town of Villiputuvai,
she of excellence
whose eyebrows arch like a bow,
poured out her intense longing for
the radiant light of Āyarpāṭi
the lord who brought her pain.
Those who chant
these verses of praise
will never flounder
in the sea of sorrow. 10

14

We Saw Him There in Vṛindāvan
(Paṭṭi mēyntu)

Roaming at will,
that lively bull,
calf younger to Baladeva,
Laying bets
in playful freedom,
did you see him come this way?

With the cows and calves
he loves so well,
tending, grazing,
playing with them—
we saw him there in Vṛindāvan. 1

He deserted me
left me in pain.
He held Āyarpāṭi
in thrall,
that young calf
who stinks of stables,
have you seen Govardhana?

Garland of sacred basil
gleaming upon his form
like a streak of lightening
on a dark rain cloud,
playing with the cowherd crowd,
we saw him there in Vṛindāvan. 2

Nampi whose name is illusion,
that bridegroom
who enraptures all,

he who tells impossible lies
have you seen him anywhere?

Garuḍa, son of Vinata,
hovers above
wings outspread
across the sun.
Beneath that shady canopy
we saw him there in Vṛindāvan. 3

I am caught,
pulled by the noose
of the lotus eyes which gleam
in his cool dark face,
this game he plays—
have you seen that radiant lord?

Beads of sweat
glisten upon his form—
like a spotted
elephant calf,
deep in play,
we saw him there in Vṛindāvan. 4

Like the boar
escaped from its net
is Mādhavan̲, my dark–hued gem,
the lord who gives naught at all,
have you seen him come this way?

Trailing his yellow robe,
that dark calf
filled the street
like a great black cloud—
we saw him there in Vṛindāvan. 5

His eyebrows
arch in beauty
like the *sāranga* bow

he holds.
That inconsistent one,
lawless, capricious—
did you see him come this way?

Like rising sun
above the mountain top,
face glowing
upon a dark–hued form
we saw him there in Vṛindāvan. 6

Nampi who is harmony,
dark within and dark without,
who baffles our designs,
have you seen that great dark cloud?

Circled by a crowd of friends
like the midnight sky
with twinkling stars,
we saw him there in Vṛindāvan. 7

Yellow–robed one
holding aloft the discus
white conch in hand
Tirumāl, grace incarnate—
have you seen him anywhere?

Like drunken bees
his fragrant tresses
upon his shoulders
as he plays—
we saw him there in Vṛindāvan. 8

"Create the worlds!"
he said to Brahmā,
his navel lotus
he gave as home—
have you seen that immaculate lord?

That great hunter
searched the forests,
eliminated
elephant, Dhenuka, Baka—
we saw him there in Vṛindāvan. 9

Kōtai of Viṣṇucittaṉ sang
of having seen on earth
in Vṛindāvan,
the supreme lord
who saved the great elephant.
Those who meditate on these verses
as a balm
to cure all ills
will find eternal rest
at the glorious feet of the lord. 10

Notes on the Poems

1. Unite Me With My Lord, O Kāmadeva

Kāmadeva or Manmatha, is the traditional god of love, akin to Eros or Amor of Mediterranean mythology, and pictured thus:

"Ananka conquers the whole world
with his five arrows
and bow of flowers,
his bow–string a row of bees,
his general the season of Spring,
his chariot the southern Malaya breeze"
(*Saundaryalahiri*, verse 6)

Manmatha is renowned for uniting lovers. He dared to aim an arrow at Śiva engrossed in yogic meditation, to make him fall in love with Pārvatī, who was doing *tapas* (penance) to attain Śiva. Manmatha paid dearly for his arrogance; opening his third eye, Śiva burned him to ashes. (He was ultimately brought back to life through Pārvatī's intervention.)

Āṇṭāḷ's first hymn, in which she requests Manmatha to unite her with her chosen lord, appropriately sets the tone for the set of fourteen hymns. The very first verse in which Āṇṭāḷ states her inability to live without her lord, expresses her anguish at separation from her beloved. To achieve her end of union with the lord, Āṇṭāḷ invokes Manmatha by performing a *vṛata* or vow. Her reference to the fact that the entire month of Tai (mid–January to mid–February) is past, that Māci (mid–February to mid–March) has begun, and that Paṅkuni (mid–March to mid–April) is here (verse 6), confirms that the *vṛata* is performed for forty or forty-eight days as is the tradition when a vow is undertaken for a specific purpose.

Manmatha is traditionally considered to be the son of Viṣṇu and Lakṣmī. The commentary of both Periyavāccān Piḷḷai and of earlier writers alludes to Ma<u>n</u>matha's relationship as son to Āṇṭāḷ, since Āṇṭāḷ herself is regarded by worshippers as the incarnation of Bhūdevī, second consort of Viṣṇu. However, this relationship is never referred to by Āṇṭāḷ herself, and may therefore be safely ignored as it only detracts from our understanding of Āṇṭāḷ's emotional state and spiritual fervor. Though the song is a constant appeal to Ma<u>n</u>matha, Āṇṭāḷ's entire being is engrossed in meditating upon the varying forms of her dark–hued lord.

P. 75 lines 3, 6 — The months of the Tamil solar calendar occupy fixed positions in the solar year and begin around the middle of the Western months. Tai, Maci and Paṅku<u>n</u>i are the three Tamil months roughly corresponding to mid–January to mid–February, mid–February to mid–March, and mid–March to mid–April.

P. 75 line 5 — mandalas of fine sand: it is customary, in most parts of India, to decorate the threshold of one's home every morning with an auspicious diagram usually drawn with powdered rice which is sometimes mixed with water. The mandalas that Āṇṭāḷ refers to in this verse appear to be of a special variety, related to the vow she has undertaken.

P. 75 line 8 — Āṇṭāḷ offers worship to Ma<u>n</u>ṁatha and his brother. Commentator Periyavāccā<u>n</u> Piḷḷai writes in Sanskrit *namōstu rāmāya ca Lakṣmaṇāya* or "I bow to Rāma and Lakṣmaṇa," indicating that in the case of great persons it is customary to bow to the brother as well as the main deity. Periyavāccā<u>n</u> adds that Ma<u>n</u>matha's brother is Sāman.

P. 75 line 11 — Anankadeva or formless god: a reference to the fact that Śiva burned Manmatha to ashes for having dared to shoot an arrow at him.

P. 75 lines 24, 25 — lord who rent open the beak of the bird: a reference to an incident from Kṛṣṇa's boyhood days when he defeated a demon who had taken the form of a giant crane (*baka*). See note to *Tiruppāvai*, P. 50 lines 23, 24.

P. 76 line 3 — Govinda: the cowherd lord (*go* = cow; Indra = lord) or perhaps "finder of cows" (*go vinda*).

P. 76 lines 7–13 — The verse contains a complete description of Manmatha's attributes.

P. 76 line 16 — Dvārka: the town in Western India (still known by the same name) where Kṛṣṇa ruled as king, after he gave up his cowherd life.

P. 77 line 15 — Trivikrama who spanned the worlds: a reference to Viṣṇu's incarnation as the dwarf, *Vāmana,* who assumed the gigantic form of Trivikrama once he had been granted three strides of land by king Bali. For details, see note to *Tiruppāvai*, P. 44 lines 8, 9. Āṇṭāḷ makes frequent allusions to this important story from the Viṣṇu legend.

P. 77 line 23 — The full significance of Āṇṭāḷ's tangled, disheveled hair is appreciated by comparison with her description of herself in the signature verse of several of these hymns as "Kōtai of the glossy tresses", "long–haired Kōtai", or "Kōtai of the long black tresses".

Her hair, it seems, was indeed her crowning glory; but she permitted her tresses to remain uncombed for the total duration of the *vṛata* or vow that she undertook.

P. 77 line 29 Keśava : A name given to Kṛṣṇa that refers, in all likelihood, to his killing of the horse–demon Késin.

P. 78 line 14 Gajendra: king of elephants and a devotee of Viṣṇu, was once caught and dragged into the waters of a pond by a wicked crocodile. Hearing Gajendra's piteous cries for help, Viṣṇu arrived upon his divine eagle mount Garuḍa, killed the crocodile and rescued Gajendra.

P. 78 line 15 lord who broke the elephant's tusk: a reference to an incident from Kṛṣṇa legend. When the evil king Kaṃsa sent a demon in the form of the elephant Kuvalayāpīḍa, to trample and kill Kṛṣṇa and his half-brother Balarāma, Kṛṣṇa effortlessly broke the creature's tusk and then slew the elephant.

P. 78 line 16 lord who rent open the beak of the bird: a reference to Kṛṣṇa's victory over the bird–demon Baka.

2. Do Not Break Our Sandcastles

In this song which is partially in the genre of *piḷḷai–tamiḻ* (poetry on god, king, or hero as child), Āṇṭāḷ becomes one of a group of little *gopī* girls who have decorated the street with sandcastles. Boy Kṛṣṇa arrives only to tease the girls and break their sand houses, and the entire song consists of repeated appeals to him to stop playing his mischievous pranks. This *ciṟṟil* (sandcastle) song, part of a Tamil tradition, was used by the poets of the earlier Caṅkam age; Āṇṭāḷ and the Āḻvārs applied it to Kṛṣṇa legend. Periyavāccān̲'s lengthy commentary on this poem is in the nature of an imaginary conversation between Kṛṣṇa and the young girls whose sandcastles are being broken. This conversation, quite charming in its own way, attempts to fill in the gaps left by the verses.

There appears to be a deeper meaning underlying what seems to be on the surface, a delightful and amusing dialogue between Kṛṣṇa and the little *gopīs* building sandcastles. Āṇṭāḷ perhaps visualizes Kṛṣṇa's action as an attempt to attract the *gopīs* to him, to bring them to divine recollection, away from mundane preoccupations. Read as a charming interlude between the little *gopīs* and mischief making Kṛṣṇa, the hymn is attractive in its literal meaning. Incidentally, the deeper spiritual interpretation has not been mentioned by Periyavāccān̲ Piḷḷai.

P. 79 line 4 — Nārāyaṇa: a name of Viṣṇu in his role as cosmic creator, when he reclines upon the waters of the primeval ocean known as Nāra. (See also note below to P. 80 lines 2, 3.) In the Tamil-speaking areas of India this name also applies to Viṣṇu as he lay, as an infant, upon a banyan leaf that floated on the primeval ocean, sucking his left toe—a position symbolizing both self–communion and timelessness. It was after this self–communion that he decided to create the world.

P. 79 line 5 — Yaśodā: foster mother of Kṛṣṇa, who was born as son to Devakī and her husband Vasudeva. See note to *Tiruppāvai* P. 43 lines 13, 14 and P. 58 lines 1–4.

P. 79 line 7 — Paṅkun̲i: the month of the Tamil lunar calendar roughly corresponding to mid–March to mid–April.

P. 79 line 8 — Kāmadeva: god of love. The connection of this *cir̲r̲il* song to the first hymn addressed to Ma<u>n</u>matha is evident from the remark of the *gopīs* that their castles are part of the street decoration to herald the arrival of Kāmadeva.

P. 79 line 9 — Śrīdhara: A name of Viṣṇu meaning "upholder of goddess Srī."

P. 79 lines 19, 20 — You slept upon the banyan leaf. See note to P. 79 line 4 on Nārāyaṇa.

P. 80 lines 2, 3 — You who slumber upon the surging ocean: a reference to Viṣṇu in his form as cosmic creator, as he lay reclining upon the serpent Ananta who floated upon the waters of the primeval ocean. It is a time prior to the emergence of the lotus from Viṣṇu's navel—the lotus that housed Brahmā who then created the worlds.

P. 80 line 20 — Mādhava: name of Kṛṣṇa. The etymology is somewhat uncertain but may derive from *madhu* meaning "springtime" or "honey."

P. 80 lines 32–35 — A reference to Viṣṇu, in his incarnation as Rāma, the great warrior of Laṅkā, who crossed the ocean and destroyed whole clans of demons.

P. 81 lines 8, 9 — The young *gopīs* remind Kṛṣṇa that, as Rāma, he was the builder of the bridge to Laṅkā; they ask if it is fair that the "builder" of the bridge should "break" their sand–buildings.

P. 81 lines 29–31 — lord who once spanned the earth and measured the worlds; a reference to Trivikrama.

P. 82 lines 1–4 A clear demonstration of the manner in which Kṛṣṇa and other forms of Viṣṇu are intermingled in Āṇṭāḷ's imagination. The little *gopī* girls (part of Kṛṣṇa legend alone) beseech the lord who once tasted the nectar of Sītā's lips (the Rāma incarnation), not to destroy their play houses of sand.

P. 82 line 7 Vaikuṇṭa: the heaven of Viṣṇu.

3. Give Back Our Clothes

This song celebrates the famous episode in which Kṛṣṇa steals the clothes of the *gopīs* while they are bathing in the stream. Here Āṇṭāḷ visualizes herself as one of the young girls who falls prey to the pranks of young Kṛṣṇa. Attempting to draw a connection from one hymn to the next, Periyavāccā<u>n</u> Piḷḷai suggests that the young *gopīs* go to plunge in the cold waters of the pond in order to appease the fire of longing that had arisen in them as the result of Kṛṣṇa's touch, evidenced in verse nine of the previous hymn two. It is of relevance to note, as our commentator points out, that the phrase *cu<u>n</u>ai–āṭal* or "plunging in the waters" is a euphemism for "sexual union."

The inner significance of the story lies in its stress on the need for complete surrender, a total effacement of the self if one is to attain the lord and realize him. Physical nakedness is a way of conveying an utter lack of body–consciousness, a state of pristine purity. Yet when Kṛṣṇa makes this the condition, the *gopīs* are not prepared to abandon all and come face to face with their god.

It is perhaps the Kannada woman poet–saint Mahādeviyakkā who, three centuries after Āṇṭāḷ, expressed and demonstrated the totally external nature of clothing for one who seeks identification with the Soul or Self. Abandoning clothes herself, Mahādeviyakkā went around wrapped only in her long tresses, as a concession to the sensibilities of those around her, rather than from any felt need to cover herself. See Ramanujan (1973):112–113.

"When all the world is the eye of the lord,
onlooking everywhere, what can you
cover and conceal?"

(A.K. Ramanujan. (1973):131)

P. 83 line 11, 12 — my friend and I raise a hand to beseech you: the young girls, covering their nakedness with one hand, raise the other hand, and together form the *anjali mudrā* in a gesture of prayer.

P. 83 line 16 — Māl: also Tirumāl (sacred Māl): the ancient (Caṅkam poetry) appellation for Viṣṇu. In essence, the name means "great god."

P. 83 line 20 — Māyan: a name of Kṛṣṇa; lord of illusion.

P. 83 lines 21, 23 — *That* is not in our destiny/*that* we will not do: I have retained the ambiguity of Āṇṭāḷ's original (*viti-inmaiyāl-atu māṭōm*); Periyavāccān Piḷḷai states categorically that the word "*atu*" or "that" refers to *samśleṣa* or embrace and union.

P. 83 lines 24, 25 — Leaped and danced upon the serpent's head: the story of Kṛṣṇa subduing the serpent Kāliya whose poison caused the waters of the Yamunā river to boil. Climbing high upon a *katampa* oak tree, Kṛṣṇa dived into the waters and wrestled with Kāliya until he had mastered him; he then danced a triumphal dance upon the many–hooded serpent head.

P. 84 lines 2–5 — This verse is another instance of the manner in which Kṛṣṇa and other forms of Viṣṇu exist side by side in Āṇṭāḷ's consciousness. The *gopīs* (part of the Kṛṣṇa avatar story) beseech Rāma who destroyed Laṅkā with his bow (the previous avatar), to return them their clothes.

P. 84 lines 31–33 the lotus has a spiny stem.

P. 85 lines 9, 10 lord who alone exists at the deluge: a reference to Viṣṇu's incarnation as the fish, *Matsya,* to save Manu, the ancestor of all man, from being destroyed in the universal deluge that swept over the earth. See O'Flaherty (1975):179–184.

P. 85 line 14 *māmī* = aunt. The significance of this remark emerges from the fact that marriage between cousins was the accepted norm in the Tamil country; Kṛṣṇa's teasing of these girls was therefore understandable. Āṇṭāḷ however tells Kṛṣṇa that among the girls he is teasing are many who are not his cousins, but strangers.

P. 85 line 25 Kaṃsa. See note to *Tiruppāvai*, p. 43 lines 13, 14. Vasudeva and Devakī were in prison when Kṛṣṇa was born. Miraculously Vasudeva's fetters fell off, the guards succumbed to a deep sleep, thus enabling Vasudeva, in the dead of night, to carry infant Kṛṣṇa in a basket to the home of Yaśodā and Nanda, and there secretly carry out the exchange of infants. Back in Mathurā, Vasudeva replaced his fetters, the city gates closed of their own accord, the guards awoke, and Kaṃsa was none the wiser.

P. 85 lines 31, 32 deceitful ghoul: a reference to demoness Pūtanā who, taking the form of a gracious woman, gave her poisonous breast milk to

Kṛṣṇa to suck. See note to *Tiruppāvai*, P. 46 lines 10, 11.

P. 86 line 3 Nampi: lord; name of Kṛṣṇa.

4. Join Up, O *Kūṭal*

The *Kūṭal*, a popular game among young girls in South India, requires that the players circumscribe a circle on the ground keeping their eyes closed. If a complete circle is formed (if the *kūṭal* joins up) the belief is that their wishes will come true; if however the two ends do not meet, their wishes will remain unfulfilled. The game appears to date back to early times. One of the hymns of the seventh century Śaiva saint, Appar, also refers to this popular game. See Francois Gros and T.V. Gopal Iyer, eds. *Tēvāram: Hymnes Śivaïtes du pays Tamoul. Volume 2: Appar et Cuntarar* (Pondicherry: Institut Français d'Indologie, vol 5, hymn 88, verse 8, (1985):198. In this song Āṇṭāḷ begs the *kūṭal* game itself to prophecy her union with the lord.

P. 87 line 5 Māliruñcōlai: literally "dark grove of Māl," is the ancient name of the town Aḻakarkoil, some fifty miles from Srīvilliputtūr, birth place of Āṇṭāḷ.

P. 87 line 7 Āṇṭāḷ's wish that she should be the one to touch and soothe the feet of Viṣṇu is a significant request. This particular service is reserved for Śrī or Lakṣmī, and indeed in numerous images of reclining Viṣṇu one sees Lakṣmī seated at his feet. It is the ultimate in personal service and Āṇṭāḷ's very first wish in the *kūṭal* game.

P. 87 line 9 Vēṅkaṭa: the sacred hill known today as Tirupati.

P. 87 line 12 Kaṇṇapuram: literally town of Kaṇṇaṉ, which is Tamil for Kṛṣṇa.

P. 87 lines 18, 19 Devakī and Vasudeva, the true parents of Kṛṣṇa. See notes to *Tiruppāvai*, P. 43 lines 13, 14 and P. 58 lines 1–4.

P. 87 line 27 Kāliya: See above note to P. 83 lines 24, 25. See also O'Flaherty (1975):221–228.

P. 87 line 30 Maturai (Madurai) is the orthographic equivalent of Mathurā, the city in Northern India associated with Kṛṣṇa.

P. 88 line 3 Wild elephant: See previous note to P. 78 line 15.

P. 88 lines 4, 5 The word *kūṭal* which means "joining, coming together," also indicates the confluence of rivers, and is further used to signify sexual union. The varying uses of the word *kūṭal*, as also its use as both noun and verb, is well illustrated by the last line of this verse:

Kūṭumākil nī kūṭiṭu kūṭale
If he will unite with me
then join, O *kūṭal*

P. 88 line 8 split the *maruta* trees. The toddler Kṛṣṇa is well–known as the butter thief who ate the fresh butter that mother Yaśodā had just churned. As punishment, Yaśodā tied him to the mortar. Kṛṣṇa however dragged the mortar along with him and when it got wedged between two *maruta* trees, he pulled more firmly making the trees come crashing down. In Sanskrit literature the tree involved in this episode is described as the *arjuna*, a forest tree with fragrant flowers.

P. 88 line 14 Śiśupāla: This is a story of Kṛṣṇa's post-cowherd days when he ruled Dvārka, and

refers to his carrying off princess Rukmiṇī,
daughter of the king of Kundināpura,
whose marriage had been arranged to
Śiśupāla, king of the Chēdis. Rukmiṇī, who
had lost her heart to Kṛṣṇa, sent a message
to him and he appeared on the wedding
day and abducted Rukmiṇī in front of
guards and assembled guests. Pursuing
armies were kept at bay by Kṛṣṇa's half—
brother, Balarāma, and at Dvārka, Kṛṣṇa
married Rukmiṇī.

P. 88 line 16   killed the seven bulls: a reference to a
South Indian legend in which Kṛṣṇa won
his cowherd wife Piṉṉai by slaying seven
demons in the guise of bulls who had
invaded the herd of Piṉṉai's father Kumb-
haka, brother to Yaśodā, Kṛṣṇa's foster
mother.

P. 88 line 17   the great bird: Bakāsura. See previous note
to P. 78 line 16.

P. 88 line 18   killed powerful Kaṃsa: having foiled
Kaṃsa's many attempts to destroy him,
Kṛṣṇa finally killed Kaṃsa by walking up to
his throne, and knocking him senseless in
front of his entire court.

P. 88 line 26   Dvārka: town in western India where
Kṛṣṇa ruled as king.

P. 89 line 3   He saved the tortured elephant: a reference to the story of Gajendra. See previous
note to P. 78 line 14.

5. Koelbird, Call Him To Me

This song in which Āṇṭāḷ sends the black koel (the Indian
cuckoo) as her messenger of love, is an established mode of

Sanskrit love poetry, and was adopted by Tamil poetry. The hymn is Āṇṭāḷ's cry of anguish, the anguish of separation and loneliness, set in contrast against the koel's companionship with its mate, dwelling in green groves of beauty. This is expressed in differing ways in its various verses, as Āṇṭāḷ describes her love–sickness, suffering and loneliness, while the fortunate koelbird enjoys all that she lacks.

P. 91 lines 8, 9 — Bangles slipping off wrists is a standard motif used in Tamil poetry, and to a lesser degree in Sanskrit literature, to indicate the love–sick condition. The pangs of love have left the young girl so emaciated that her slender wrists can no longer retain the bangles. Āṇṭāḷ plays with this theme in several hymns, most notably in hymn eleven.

P. 91 lines 31–33 & P. 92 line 1 — A reference to the great battle between Rāma (who rode Indra's chariot drawn by Indra's charioteer Mātali), and the many–headed demon–king Ravaṇa, in which as Rāma felled head after head, a new one grew in its place.

P. 92 line 15 — Vaikuṇṭa, the name of Viṣṇu's heaven, is here visualized as a ship that will carry Āṇṭāḷ across the world of sorrow to the bliss of Viṣṇu.

P. 92 line 25 — Villiputtūr: Āṇṭāḷ's hometown; the temple houses a reclining image of Viṣṇu.

P. 92 line 27 — carp–shaped eyes were considered to be the epitome of beauty.

P. 92 line 31 — pet parrot: in view of the fact that Āṇṭāḷ is frequently depicted in sculpture and painting with a parrot perched upon her hand, it is interesting to note her reference to her pet parrot.

P. 92 line 37 Hṛṣikeśa: a name of Viṣṇu; generally understood to mean "lord of the senses."

P. 93 line 13 The surging cosmic waters upon which Viṣṇu slumbers are often referred to as a milky ocean.

P. 93 lines 28–36 This verse contains several phrases left intentionally ambiguous by Āṇṭāḷ. Periyavāccāṉ Piḷḷai's commentary spells it out for us in black–and–white. He informs us that the vow taken by Āṇṭāḷ and her lord was to the effect that neither would live without the other. He does not care to leave the reader to form his own opinion as to what Āṇṭāḷ will do to her lord; instead he informs us that she will retaliate for the heartache caused her, and that her retaliation would be akin to putting food before a starving person and then removing it abruptly. Periyavāccāṉ further suggests that the koelbird has been a secret witness to Āṇṭāḷ's earlier intimacy with the lord, and it is hence that she chose the melodious bird as her messenger.

P. 94 line 17 The moon and the southern breeze are traditionally connected with love and lovers.

6. I Dreamt This Dream, My Friend

This simple and attractive hymn re–enacts, verse by verse, all the marriage rites, with the last line of each verse repeating that Āṇṭāḷ saw the scene in a dream. This popular sixth hymn of Āṇṭāḷ's *Tirumoḻi* is regularly recited to this day at all Vaiṣṇava weddings in South India. One scholar comments on "the glaring omission of the *tāli*," the emblem of the married state, put around the bride's neck by the bridegroom. See C. and H. Jesudasan, *A History of Tamil Literature*, Calcutta: YMCA Publishing House, (1961):110. However, the nonmention of this all–important rite in Āṇṭāḷ's dream wedding has a very simple explanation. The *tāli* rite became a part of South Indian marriages only from the eleventh century, at least two hundred years after Āṇṭāḷ, being mentioned first in the *Kanda Purānam*, the Kamban̲ *Rāmāvatāram* and other texts of this date. See C. Jayadev, "Literary and Ethnographic References to the Tali and the Tali Rite," *Transactions of the Archaeological Society of South India*, 1959–60:43–71. It is not mentioned in the marriage of the seventh century Śaiva saint Campantar, or the wedding of eighth century Śaiva saint Cuntarar, and its nonmention in Āṇṭāḷ's dream wedding has no special significance. The dream song indicates that the grace of God will surely descend upon Āṇṭāḷ, since the lord allowed her to visualize him as a bridegroom.

P. 95 line 4 Nāraṇa Nampi: name of Viṣṇu.

P. 95 line 8 golden urn: a water vessel full of leaves is considered an auspicious emblem.

P. 96 line 16 Madhusūdana: name of Viṣṇu meaning Killer of (the demon) Madhu. The story is part of the cosmic myth when two demons, Madhu and Kaitabha, sprang from the ear of Viṣṇu who was slumbering on the cosmic ocean upon the serpent couch Ananta. Their aim was to attack Brahmā who had just emerged from Viṣṇu's navel lotus; Viṣṇu woke in time to slay them.

P. 96 line 34 *ammī*: a flat stone for grinding pastes from herbs and spices. During the marriage ceremony, the bride's foot is placed upon such a stone.

P. 97 line 6 Acutan̲: name of Viṣṇu; literally "imperishable one."

7. White Conch From The Fathomless Sea

Āṇṭāḷ's fleeting dream experience of the marriage ceremony left her longing even more for her chosen lord, and in this song she addresses the conch shell which rests in Viṣṇu's left hand and which he would raise to his lips to blow. She queries the conch about the fragrance and the flavor of the lips of Mādhava, envies its power and position and its intimacy with the lord. Periyavāccāṉ Piḷḷai suggests that the first verse of the song should be understood as a refrain, to be repeated after each of the following verses.

P. 99 line 17 & P. 100 line 11 — Pañcacaṉa (demon) and Pāñcacanya (Viṣṇu's conch shell). The wicked demon Pañcacaṉa, who had taken refuge in the ocean, was killed by Kṛṣṇa who then used the shell, into which the demon had transformed himself, as a horn with which to arouse and frighten other demons. Viṣṇu's conch is hence known as Pāñcacanya.

P. 99 line 30 — Vāsudeva: name of Krsna; literally (son) "of Vasudeva."

P. 99 line 31 — Vaṭa–Maturai, "Northern Maturai" is the term used for the city of Mathurā in North India.

P. 100 line 2 — Valampurī conch: Viṣṇu's sacred conch with its spirals ṭurning towards the right. See note to *Tiruppāvai*, P. 45 line 8.

P. 100 line 4 — Dāmodara: A name of Kṛṣṇa; literally in Sanskrit "One with a rope tied around his belly." The name refers to the time that mother Yaśodā tied young Kṛṣṇa to a mortar for stealing the butter she had just churned. See also previous note to hvmn P. 88 line 8.

P. 100 line 20 *tīrtha*: holy site, holy waters.

P. 101 line 9 16,000 *devīs*: a reference to the many wives/loves of Kṛṣṇa.

P. 101 line 21 Padmanābhā: a name of Viṣṇu; literally "He with the lotus in his navel," referring to the creation myth in which a lotus containing the god Brahmā grows out of Viṣṇu's navel while that great lord is slumbering on his serpent couch that floats on the waters of the cosmic ocean. Brahmā is allotted the task of creating the worlds.

8. O Dark Rain Clouds

In this song Āṇṭāḷ sees her beloved as the lord of Vēṅkaṭa (modern sacred Tirupati), and asks the rain clouds that hover above Vēṅkaṭa Hill whether they have brought her word from him. She requests them to go tell the lord of Vēṅkaṭa about her forlorn condition and her anguish at separation.

Periyavāccāṉ Piḷḷai's commentary on this song, as indeed on those to follow, brings in many comparisons to incidents from the *Rāmāyaṇa*, especially to Sītā's separation from Rāma. It appears that he would make us understand Āṇṭāḷ and her longing for her dark lord Kṛṣṇa by comparing her anguish to that of Sītā. Presumably he fears that a young woman's expression in physical terms of the inner mystical approach to the beloved may otherwise be misunderstood. Periyavāccāṉ Piḷḷai compares Āṇṭāḷ's condition to Sītā's torment when, on the island of Laṅkā, disheveled and unornamented, she bewails the absence of Rāma and her own isolation. He suggests that the mental and emotional states of Āṇṭāḷ and Sītā are comparable. By this means he seems to justify Āṇṭāḷ's fervor and her self–assumed position as bride of the lord. By pointing to Āṇṭāḷ as Sītā's counterpart, he makes it possible for Āṇṭāḷ's attitude to her lord to be accepted by the most traditional of devotees.

Another dimension to the analogy between Sītā and Āṇṭāḷ is that traditionally both are said to be incarnations of Bhūdevī (earth). According to legend, Sītā was found by Janaka (her adoptive father) in a furrow of earth in a newly ploughed field, while Āṇṭāḷ was discovered by Viṣṇucitta (her adoptive father) beneath a *tulasī* (sacred basil) bush.

P. 103 line 24 — the southern breeze is one of the traditional accompaniments of the love–lorn condition. Ordinarily the southern breeze as opposed to the chill northern wind is warm and pleasant, but for one plagued by love–sickness, even the soothing southern breeze only brings in torturing thoughts of the absent beloved.

P. 103 line 26 — The reference to bracelets and anklets slipping off is part of the traditional Tamil imagery for the lovelorn condition.

P. 103 lines 31, 32 — This verse is yet another instance of the manner in which Kṛṣṇa and Viṣṇu are intertwined in Āṇṭāḷ's imagination. She speaks of sending word to Govinda (the cowherd lord Kṛṣṇa) who lives in Vēṅkaṭa (sacred southern Tirupati, which has no connection with the Kṛṣṇa legend).

P. 104 lines 5, 6 — Viṣṇu's consort, the goddess Śrī (Lakṣmī) is visualized as being constantly with her lord.

P. 104 line 18 — lord who killed Hiraṇya: a reference to Viṣṇu's incarnation as Narasimha (man–lion). Hiraṇyakaśipu had received a boon from Brahmā which specified that he could be killed by neither man nor beast, neither in earth or in heaven, neither by day nor by night, nor by the use of any known weapon. In this invincible position, his power threatened and rivaled that of the gods. In order to destroy him, Viṣṇu took the form of Narasimha (neither man nor beast), held him up in the air (neither heaven nor earth), killed him at twilight (neither day nor night), and used his lion claws to disembowel him (not a conventional weapon).

P. 105 line 7 — lord who churned the conch–laden ocean: a reference to Viṣṇu's assumption of the form of the tortoise, and the churning of the cosmic ocean by the gods and demons, in order to recover various treasures lost in the great deluge. See note to *Tiruppāvai* P. 61 lines 5, 6.

P. 105 lines 19, 20 — Great lord of victory; hero of the battlefield: a reference to the exploits of Rāma in Laṅkā.

P. 105 line 25 — What more suitable for comparison with Āṇṭāḷ's dry agony than the withered *erukku* leaf, the *erukku* being a milky shrub.

9. In The Grove Of My Lord

Āṇṭāḷ is so totally absorbed in divine meditation and in thoughts of the lord that everything in the grove of Māliruñcōlai recalls to her the glow of Kṛṣṇa's face, the dark color of his form, the depth and beauty of his eyes and his pearly smile. Māliruñcōlai or "dark grove of Māl" is the ancient name of Aḻakarkoil (near Maturai), some fifty miles from Śrīvilliputtūr, the birthplace of Āṇṭāḷ. From the season of the rains in the preceding hymn which is addressed to the dark rain clouds, we move on to the Indian spring, the season of berries and blossoms. We might perhaps infer that the change in seasons is symbolic of a new phase in Āṇṭāḷ's seemingly slow, yet definite progress on her inner spiritual journey towards the lord.

P. 109 lines 30–34 The significance of Āṇṭāḷ comparing herself to the cassia blossoms emerges only with the knowledge that while the buttercup tree is sacred to her lord Viṣṇu, the cassia is intimately connected with god Śiva who wears cassia blossoms in his hair. Golden cassia garlands are then of no use in a grove dedicated to Viṣṇu, and Āṇṭāḷ compares herself to them because, in the absence of the lord's grace descending upon her, she feels as useless in his grove as Śiva's cassia blossoms.

10. Thirsting For The Lord

In this song Āṇṭāḷ has reached a stage in which her mind can harbor no thoughts other than the lord. She sees him everywhere—in the mangrove flowers, the *kōvai* fruit, the jasmine creeper, the dancing peacocks, the rain–laden clouds and even the heaving ocean.

P. 111 line 32

> He speaks only one language
> says but one word.

Periyāḻvār wrote thus of the lord in his *Periyā Tirumoḻi*. Periyavāccāṉ suggests that Āṇṭāḷ's lament that the lord is double–tongued is provoked by her memory of these words.

P. 112 lines 6, 7 whose brother cut the nose of the evil ghoul: a reference to Rāma, whose brother Lakṣmaṇa cut off the nose of the giant demoness Sūrpanakha who fell in love with Lakṣmaṇa and attacked Sītā when Lakṣmaṇa rejected her.

P. 112 line 26 Kaṇṇaṉ: Tamil for Kṛṣṇa.

P. 112 line 24 & P. 113 lines 7, 8 — Verses six and seven, both addressed to the dancing peacocks, reveal the fluctuations of Āṇṭāḷ's emotions. In verse six Āṇṭāḷ finds the form of the peacocks so reminiscent of her lord that she prostrates before them as she would to the lord. In verse seven she tells the peacocks that the lord has so tortured her that she is now immune to any further torment that they might inflict upon her.

P. 113 lines 10, 11 — contains an interesting reference to the process of bronze–casting in which a wax image is enclosed in clay and then fired to form a mold into which molten metal is poured. Āṇṭāḷ visualizes the rain clouds as being like clay outside and liquid wax within. She also compares the lord to dark clay and herself to wax that will melt when embraced by her lord.

P. 113 lines 20–31 — Verse nine is addressed to the billowing ocean and refers to Viṣṇu churning the ocean. See note to *Tiruppāvai* P. 61 lines 5, 6. Āṇṭāḷ indicates that since the ocean suffered all the stages of sorrow she has endured, it should well understand her position and would thus be an appropriate messenger to the lord. Sexual imagery and terminology abound in this verse, and barely need comment. The churning of the ocean and the churning of Āṇṭāḷ's heart and soul, both entered by the lord, are described by the word *manthana*. This is a term used in the context of sexual union; *manthana*, the churning movement, is one of the modes of sexual intercourse (*Kāmasūtra*, chapter 8, *sūtra* 13). The connotation is inescapable, but also understandable, since sexual terminology, which is particularly appropriate in a spiritual context, has been used repeatedly through the centuries to explain the nature of spiritual union.

P. 113 lines 32–37 & P. 114 lines 1–3

Verse ten ends on a note of resignation. Spiritually speaking, it may be said that progress is often not apparent, frequently reaching a plateau upon which it alternates between despair and renewed longing. Āṇṭāḷ feels that perhaps her father Viṣṇucitta might succeed in evoking the lord for her, using his own method of approach which is quite different from hers. At the end of strenuous effort, she realizes that grace is necessary—that the lord must reveal himself—and so quiet seems to descend upon her.

11. He Has Taken All

In this song Āṇṭāḷ visualizes her beloved as the lord of Araṅkam (Śrīraṅkam). She expresses surprise at his neglect of her, especially since he has battled against odds for the women he loved—as Rāma who rent apart the ocean for Sītā (verse 7), as the boar Varāha who took that lowly form for the earth maiden, Bhūdevī (verse 8), and as Kṛṣṇa who claimed Rukminī as his own (verse 9). In the first six verses, Āṇṭāḷ dwells on the lord of Araṅkam as the one who has taken away her bangles and appropriated all that she possesses. In this context, we must remember that woman's wealth, in the form of dowry, was represented by her jewelry (here, her bangles). Āṇṭāḷ sees the inappropriateness of the fact that the Supreme lord of the worlds should have stolen her small riches. Yet, at the same time, Āṇṭāḷ meditates upon him as the all–pervasive lord and as the essence of the Vedas (verse 6).

As indicated earlier, South Indian poetry, from the Caṅkam period onwards, regularly utilized the motif of bangles slipping off the wrists to indicate a girls' love–sick condition in which pining for her beloved has made her so thin that the bangles no longer remain upon her wrist. When Āṇṭāḷ says that the beloved has "taken all," she implies that she has emptied herself to enable him to fulfill her. The significance of this entire hymn rests upon this "taking of all," symbolized by the bangles slipping off her wrists. Though Āṇṭāḷ is thinking of her bangles as the only little outer wealth left to her, she also refers to her utter inner poverty, in which "all is nothing" without the lord, and in which she feels so empty that the lord must perforce fill her.

P. 115 line 12 — fire–tongued serpent: Ananta who coils himself to form a couch for Viṣṇu.

P. 116 lines 20, 21 — deceptive (*pollā*) form of the dwarf: see note to *Tiruppāvai* P. 44 lines 8, 9. Periyavāccāṉ, one might note, disliked the use of the adjective "deceptive" and made the ingenious suggestion that the word *pollā* should, in this instance, be interpreted as "beautiful."

P. 117 lines 5–8 — A reference to Viṣṇu's incarnation as Rāma, his deep distress at the abduction of Sītā, and his unceasing search for her culminating in fording the ocean to Laṅkā and finally defeating and killing Rāvaṇa.

P. 117, lines 13–18 — A reference to Viṣṇu's incarnation as the great boar Varāha, in which form he rescued the goddess earth (Bhūdevī) who was submerged in the depths of the cosmic ocean, and lifted her up to glory. The goddess earth became Viṣṇu's love and his second consort, being popularly known as Bhū Lakṣmī to distinguish her from Śrī Lakṣmī. See O'Flaherty (1975):184–197.

P. 117 lines 24–32 — The story of Kṛṣṇa carrying off the princess Rukminī, whose wedding to

Śiśupāla was about to take place, and then marrying her in Dvārka. See previous note to P. 88 line 14.

P. 118 lines 1, 2 — It is likely that this is a reflection of Kṛṣṇa's words to Arjuna (*Bhagavadgītā*, chapter 7, verse 17) to the effect that those who come to him with single-minded love and devotion are exceedingly dear to him. A similar sentiment is also voiced in *Bhagavadgītā*, chapter 12, verses 14–20.

12. Take Me To The Land Of My Lord

"I must go to him—take me to his dwelling-places" is the refrain of this song, marking yet another step forward in Āṇṭāḷ's inner journey. She yearns to set foot upon the earth hallowed by the footprints of Kṛṣṇa. Starting with Mathurā, in succeeding verses she longs to be at the various sites sacred to the story of Kṛṣṇa: in Gokula, Nandagōpa's home, the banks of the Yamunā where Kṛṣṇa killed Kāliya, the foot of the sacred banyan tree at Bāndiram where the asura Pralamba was overcome, Bhaktavilōcana, Govardhana, and finally the city of Dvārka.

P. 119 lines 6–8 — The words you utter/are like the deaf/ speaking to the dumb: a colloquialism—*ūmaiyarōṭu ceviṭar vārtai*.

P. 119 line 12 — The warring Mallas: the reference is to the great wrestling match at Mathurā in which the evil King Kaṃsa pitted his most powerful wrestlers against Kṛṣṇa and Balarāma; the match immediately preceded the killing of Kaṃsa by Kṛṣṇa.

P. 120 lines 21, 22 — I have understood the phrase *Govindanuk–allāl–vāyil–pōkā*, referring to Āṇṭāḷ's breasts, as meaning "they are meant only for Govinda's mouth," although I have used a less literal translation. The word *vāy–il* means "into the mouth" or "the threshold" (of a home). Since Āṇṭāḷ speaks in this verse of her breasts clad in a red bodice, that hide their eyes (nipples) and draw back in shame at the sight of mere mortals, and since various other verses express Āṇṭāḷ's longing for the caress of the lord, it appears that the more literal interpretation is indicated. The idea of "the threshold of Govinda's home" seems forced. One may note that Āṇṭāḷ used the word *vāy–il* to mean "in the mouth" in verse four of the next song, when she asks for the nectar from the mouth of the lord; also, she uses the word *kaṭaitalai* (verse three of this song) when she refers to "the threshold (of Nandagōpa's home)."

P. 121 line 15 — Bhaktavilōcana: a reference to an episode in which a hungry and tired Kṛṣṇa and his companions went to ask for food at a place where the brahmins were performing a sacrifice. The brahmins turned down their request, whereupon Kṛṣṇa told the cowherds to approach the priests' wives, who were more receptive to the message of Kṛṣṇa and brought them generous quantities of food.

P. 121 lines 32, 33 — Demon Pralamba took the form of a cowherd and joined the cowherd coterie of Kṛṣṇa and Balarāma who were playing the game of carrying one another on their shoulders. As they reached a banyan tree at Bāndiram, Pralamba, who had Balarāma on his shoulders, assumed his true form and soared into the sky planning to take Balarāma captive. Balarāma, however, struck him such a harsh blow that the demon fell dead upon the earth.

P. 122 line 2 He was bound to the mortar. See previous note to P. 88 line 8.

P. 122 lines 8–12 Holding in victory/the mountain as umbrella: Kṛṣṇa persuaded the cowherds to worship the mountain Govardhana rather than Indra, god of thunder and rain. In his fury, Indra sent down a torrential rainstorm that threatened to sweep away the inhabitants of Gokula. Quickly Kṛṣṇa lifted up the mountain Govardhana with one hand, and held it up as a sheltering umbrella.

13. The Agony Of Desire

Āṇṭāḷ's anguish reaches a peak in this hymn, in which she begs those around her to bring her something that Kṛṣṇa wears upon his person; this alone, she feels, will have the power to soothe and revive her. Her request starts with the yellow silken robe of Kṛṣṇa and his *tulasī* garland, climaxing with the request for the nectar of the mouth of the lord. Heartbroken, she ultimately threatens to pluck out her breasts by their very roots and fling them at Kṛṣṇa's chest. This perhaps may soothe the fire that consumes her tortured heart. In the context of her dire threat, one cannot but recollect the well-known tale of Kannakī, the heroine of the fifth century Tamil epic *Cilappatikāram*, who plucked out her breasts and flung them onto the streets of Maturai where her husband Kōvalan had been unjustly executed. There can be little doubt that Āṇṭāḷ must have had this episode in mind when she made her dire threat. Dennis Hudson (forthcoming) further points out that Kannakī is actually referred to in the *Cilappatikāram* as Kōtai, and he places before us the further parallel between Kannakī's husband, Kōvalan, and Kṛṣṇa as Kōvalan (one who tends cows).

The ninth verse is an anticlimax which seems to suggest an

attitude of resignation. If the lord will fold her to himself and accept her as his bride, she would be overjoyed. Else he should look her in the eye and tell her to go her way; she would accept that decision too. Āṇṭāḷ seems to express her realization that she can never find fulfillment by her own efforts alone, and that it is necessary that the lord's grace descend upon her.

P. 123 lines 9, 10 — *Puṇṇil puḷi peytāṟ pōla*: a colloquial phrase, literally "like pouring tamarind juice into a sore." I have translated it as "sour juice/ poured upon an open wound."

P. 123 line 28 — That dancer with the waterpots: a Tamil legend, known already to the fifth century Tamil epic *Cilappatikāram*, but unknown to the Sanskrit tradition. In South India, the episode is added to a story of Kṛṣṇa legend that is common to both traditions. Uśā, daughter of the demon–king Bāna who was a devotee of god Śiva, fell in love with Kṛṣṇa's grandson, Aniruddha. Bāna disapproved of their love and imprisoned Aniruddha, and on coming to his rescue, Kṛṣṇa found he had to face Śiva who arrived to aid his devotee Bāna. Finally Kṛṣṇa defeated Śiva and Bāna in a great battle; they relented and Uśā married Aniruddha. The Tamil tradition relates that prior to this victorious battle, Kṛṣṇa danced with the waterpots in the streets of Sonilpur. The Sanskrit tradition does not know of this waterpot episode.

P. 123 line 29 — Kuṭantai: the town of Kumpakōṇam, near Tanjavur.

14. We Saw Him There In Vṛindāvan

After the intensity of hymn thirteen, this closing song is comparatively lighthearted with a rhythmic lilt of its own which

I have been unable to replicate in English. Āṇṭāḷ adopts a question–and–answer style in which it is not quite clear whether she is querying some other person, or whether she herself is answering her own questions. After the calm that descended in the ninth verse of the previous hymn, following upon the parched agony of the earlier songs, Āṇṭāḷ seems to have found a degree of fulfillment in which she keeps having visions of Kṛṣṇa as he appeared in the holy Vṛindāvan of his childhood days.

P. 127 line 5 Baladeva: Kṛṣṇa's half–brother, also called Balarāma.

P. 129 lines 2, 10 A seeming paradox arises when Āṇṭāḷ refers to Kṛṣṇa as *poruttam–ili* (verse 6) or inconsistent/incompatible One, and then as *poruttam–uṭaya* (verse 7) or the consistent/compatible One. Since the word *poruttam* is applied to the Supreme, it must be taken to mean "that which harmonizes with." Āṇṭāḷ must have visualized the lord as devoid of this quality only because he does not come to her despite her agonized longing. At the same time, with Āṇṭāḷ's capacity to view the lord as Formless, she understands that he is the very core of harmony, harmonizing with all. She cannot but call him *poruttam–uṭaya–nampi*. This is a concept difficult to express briefly in poetic English; therefore I have refrained from repeating one particular English word, since it might result in a loss of the subtlety of the original.

P. 130 line 4 elephant: Kuvalayāpīḍa: See previous note to P. 78 line 15.

P. 130 line 4 Dhenuka: a reference to a Krsna legend in which his half–brother Balarāma killed the demon Dhenuka who, taking the form of an ass, terrified the cowherd clan. Balarāma grasped the ass–demon by his hind feet and hurled him onto the top of a palmyra tree where the demon died.

Appendix One

Śrīvilliputtūr Temple Inscription of 1454 A.D.

Engraved on the south wall of the *maṇḍapa* in front of the Āṇṭāḷ temple at Śrīvilliputtūr is an inscription which records the donation of a village to the temple by the Bāna chieftain Urankāvillitāsan. Our interest in the record lies in its lengthy preamble, couched in the form of a love–letter (*praṇaya-patrikā*) from Lord Raṅkanāta to Āṇṭāḷ, which quotes several phrases and even entire verses from Āṇṭāḷ's *Tiruppāvai* and *Nācciyār Tirumoḻi*. A complete translation of the record follows:

> Let this order of Śrī Raṅkanāta, the cause of the creation of the three worlds, be fulfilled.
>
> This is the love–letter we (lord Raṅkanāta) have graciously written to "Kōtai of Viṣṇucittan/master of the people of Putuvai/of storied mansions and hilly tracts."[1] We are "the light of the world whose glory is sung and spread by *siddhas*, by Veda–chanting *ṛṣis*, by devotees and ascetics."[2] In "cool Araṅkam/where live men of virtue,"[3] in our home (temple) seated on the Ariyarāyan couch, in the Cēraṉai–veṉrān pavilion, beneath the Suntara–pāṇṭiyan canopy, we (Lord Raṅkanāta) sat in darbār, graciously receiving Tumpuru, Nārata and the gods, and according them favors. In our home (temple) were assembled shepherds, cowherds, gatherers of flowers and leaves, those who sprinkle water, guardians, devotees, pandits and others who attend to our various sacred duties. From our Kōtai's home, there arrived priests, shepherds, cowherds, guardians, devout Vaiṣṇavas. Sending ahead our retinue and all close to us, we received those of her house in the manner

appropriate, and accepted in proper manner the gifts they brought.

We read the letter that she sent which was to this effect: On hearing from her friends and relatives[4] that we were seated in the great pavilion sporting with "sixteen thousand devis,"[5] she felt the news "sting/like sour juice/ poured upon an open wound,"[6] "pierce like a dagger,"[7] make her "sore with pain, weak, worn."[8] She threatened "I shall pluck/ by their roots these useless breasts/I shall fling them at his chest/I shall cool/the raging fire within me,"[9] and she said that her "soul melts in anguish."[10] She described us as "inconsistent one,"[11] "dark within and dark without,"[12] "him who knows not/the sorrow of women,"[13] a wicked bandit, great illusory one, "the lord whose couch is the serpent/is double–tongued like his own serpent/unfortunate one that I am."[14] Since she was "from *māmī's* house,"[15] and we were from the cousin's side,[16] and since she spoke of "quarreling and uniting,"[17] all her words must have been uttered in order to derive pleasure from the hurt it caused me.

We were seated in the Periya–*maṇḍapa* together with the "thirty–three celestials"[18] to conduct affairs of state and remission of taxes. And we read of the piteous state in which her beloved had left her, and she reminded us that "between us we took a vow/known to none other."[19] She pointed out that:

> "Once long ago
> for the sake of the maiden earth
> forlorn in moss–ridden body,
> he took the shameful form
> of a filthy
> water–dripping boar.
> That radiant one
> famed lord of holy Araṅkam—
> the words that he spoke to me
> can never be erased
> from my mind.[20]

and that:

"Śiśupāla was resolved
to take her hand in marriage.
All of a sudden
his glow vanished,
he stood petrified.
The divine bridegroom
stepped in,
took her hand in marriage."[21]

and that she had heard "the lord of Araṅkam/who is truth."[22] And I do declare that I desire none but her.

Without causing those who come from Kōtai's house to wait, accord to them the honors that they merit. Give to Kōtai a palanquin, parasol, garlands, jewels, silks and cottons, scented substances and all else similar to mine. Also provide for the expenses of her temple kitchen, which is to be run in the same grand manner as mine. In Śaka year 1375 (Śrīmukha year), on Ekādaśi day in the *pūrvapakṣa*, on Wednesday, Uttara *nakṣatra*, the Bāna chieftain Urankāvillitāsan (also known as Mahāpali Vāṇātarāyar) donates the village of Tiṭiyan or Tiruvaraṅka–nallūr in Muṭṭanāṭu in the fertile district of Maturai. The boundaries are as follows: west—as far east as the Puttūr Hill and Vayiravan paddy field; north—as far south as Vārantūr field; east—to the west of Karumāttūr well; south—to the north of the tamarind grove and the standing stone. All flora and fauna, underground treasures, villages, and all other objects within these four boundaries are included. This order should be written on stone and on copper. Thus by the grace of the lord who inspired the *Tiruppāvai*, these words were written by Raṅkanāta–piriyaṉ, chief minister and scribe of the king.

Notes to Appendix One

1. *Nācciyār Tirumoḻi*, hymn 1, verse 10.
2. *Periya Tirumoḻi*, IV:9, verse 6.
3. *Nācciyār Tirumoḻi*, hymn 11, verse 5.
4. *Tiruppāvai*, 11.
5. *Nācciyār Tirumoḻi*, hymn 7, verse 9.
6. *Nācciyār Tirumoḻi*, hymn 13, verse 1.
7. *Nācciyār Tirumoḻi*, hymn 13, verse 2.
8. *Nācciyār Tirumoḻi*, hymn 13, verse 3.
9. *Nācciyār Tirumoḻi*, hymn 13, verse 8.
10. Idem.
11. *Nācciyār Tirumoḻi*, hymn 14, verse 6.
12. *Nācciyār Tirumoḻi*, hymn 14, verse 7.
13. *Nācciyār Tirumoḻi*, hymn 13, verse 1.
14. *Nācciyār Tirumoḻi*, hymn 10, verse 3.
15. *Nācciyār Tirumoḻi*, hymn 3, verse 8.
16. *Tiruppāvai*, 20.
17. *Nācciyār Tirumoḻi*, hymn 4, verse 11.
18. *Tiruppāvai*, 20.
19. *Nācciyār Tirumoḻi*, hymn 5, verse 8.
20. *Nācciyār Tirumoḻi*, hymn 11, verse 8.
21. *Nācciyār Tirumoḻi*, hymn 11, verse 9.
22. *Nācciyār Tirumoḻi*, hymn 11, verse 10.

Appendix Two

Periyavāccā<u>n</u> Piḷḷai, Thirteenth Century Commentator on Āṇṭāḷ

Kṛṣṇapātar, later given the title Periya–āccā<u>n</u>–piḷḷai or "Venerated great teacher," was born in the year 1228 at Seṅkanur in the Tanjavur district of Tamilnāṭu. Persecuted by the Śaivas of his village, Periyavāccān Piḷḷai fled to the refuge of the famous Viṣṇu temple at Śrīraṅkam, where he devoted his life to writing commentaries on a variety of Tamil and Sanskrit works, including the entire *Nālāyira Tivya Pirapantam*, the four thousand verses of the Āḻvārs. Periyavāccā<u>n</u> Piḷḷai is the only ancient scholar to have written a commentary on Āṇṭāḷ's *Nācciyār Tirumoḻi*.

Vaiṣṇava commentators wrote in a language referred to as Maṇipravāḷa, which is Tamil with a considerable admixture of Sanskrit words (*maṇi* = pearl:Sanskrit; *pravāḷa* = coral:Tamil), in which the sentence construction is totally Tamil. The Manipravāḷaof Periyavāccā<u>n</u> Piḷḷai appears to be in the proportion of two Tamil words to every one that is in Sanskrit. Apart from making Sanskrit words an integral part of a sentence, Periyavāccā<u>n</u> Piḷḷai also frequently inserted Sanskrit phrases and entire verses from Sanskrit sources into his writing, introducing these with the Tamil phrase *e<u>nn</u>umāpōlē* meaning "as it were," or with *e<u>n</u>kirapaṭiyē* meaning "so to say."

Periyavāccā<u>n</u> Piḷḷai's commentary is learned and highlights the extent of his scholarship as well as his knowledge of Vaiṣṇava literature and theism. Like all other commentators, he systematically takes verse by verse and comments on both their literal and their inner meaning (*uḷḷurai*); nowhere does he attempt an overall review of a poem. Periyavāccā<u>n</u> Piḷḷai's commentary on the *Tiruppāvai* captures the spirit of Āṇṭāḷ's verse, her mood, emotion and her intention in inviting her friends to go bathe in the waters, or in other words, to seek the grace of Kṛṣṇa. For instance, when the young maidens address the rain–god and requests him to rain upon them (verse 4), Periyavāccā<u>n</u> points out its inner significance as the request that Kṛṣṇa's blessings not be withheld from them, and that he shower his grace upon them like the rain cloud. Another dimension given to the poem by Periyavāccā<u>n</u> is the comparison of the rain cloud to the guru, who having himself absorbed the waters of Kṛṣṇa's grace, is now ready to shower it upon his disciples. In other songs, Periyavāccā<u>n</u>'s interpretation goes much further. Song twenty-eight seems on the surface to be a simple song in which Kṛṣṇa's cowherd friends, describing their own insignificant status, humbly beg forgiveness for having presumed intimacy with him. Analyzing this poem, Periyavāccā<u>n</u> shows that behind its simple phraseology are hidden the six quantities of the true devotee who aspires for divine grace—residing with the guru and leading a moral life, being without pride, extolling the lord, realizing one's true relationship with him, asking forgiveness, and requesting nearness with the lord. Periyavāccā<u>n</u>'s comparable comments on the other songs of the *Tiruppāvai* reveal his perception and his empathy with Āṇṭāḷ's presentation of the *pāvai* theme.

When we turn to *Nācciyār Tirumo<u>l</u>i*, this empathy seems to have thinned. Periyavāccā<u>n</u> Piḷḷai's reputation and prestige as prince of commentators (*vyākhyānacakravartin*) rests on his authoritative commentary on the four thousand Vaisnava sacred hymns, of which only 143 verses of *Nācciyār Tirumo<u>l</u>i* fall into the category of erotic or bridal mysticism. Āṇṭāḷ alone, in the fourteen connected songs of her *Nācciyār Tirumo<u>l</u>i*, expresses in the forthright terminology of sexual love her yearning for her beloved, the depth of her anguish at separation and her desire to unite with him. While several Ā<u>l</u>vārs composed occasional love poems in the *akam* genre, putting themselves in the place of women pining for their beloved lord, none of them wrote love poems in a connected series and rarely did they use any but traditional phraseology. While Periyavāccā<u>n</u>'s commentary on such love songs is both perceptive and learned, he appears to have been uncomfortable with Āṇṭāḷ's erotic expression of her wavering emotional states and her gradual inner evolution. Perhaps he found it difficult to handle Āṇṭāḷ's double–pronged emotional phraseology.

Āṇṭāḷ's *Nācciyār Tirumoḻi* hymns arouse a need to better comprehend the subtleties of her mystical path, the stony areas and the roses along the way as the soul journeys to meet the beloved. Periyavāccān̲'s main commentorial method here is a reliance on comparisons which may aid the devout worshipper, but which do not shed sufficient light on the intricacies of Āṇṭāḷ's experience. Perhaps Periyavāccān̲ Piḷḷai takes for granted a certain basic understanding of "*viraha tapa*" or "the anguish of separation," an accepted stage on the path of love.

Periyavāccān̲'s comparisons sometimes interfere with the main thread of his writing. Commenting on the opening lines of a verse (hymn 8, verse 2) addressed to the dark rain clouds, in which Āṇṭāḷ longs for the lord and inquires if he has sent word through them, Periyavāccān̲ Piḷḷai brings in the entire story of Sakuntalā, who was also restlessly awaiting word from her loved one. The circumstances of the Sakuntalā story however, are drastically different from those of Āṇṭāḷ. Sakuntalā secretly married Duśyanta, bore him a child, and did not know that he had been cursed to forget her. Periyavāccān̲ seems here to restrict himself to a comparison of feminine emotion when separated from the beloved, rather than taking into account surrounding circumstances which might change or mitigate the situation.

Occasionally, Periyavāccān̲'s comments distract our attention from the poignancy of a song. In verse seven of the hymn addressed to the rain clouds (hymn 8) Āṇṭāḷ sends a message to her lord:

> "Tell him I will survive
> only if he will stay with me
> for one day."

Periyavāccān̲ remarks that Āṇṭāḷ feels that since she has no indication as to when the lord will arrive, she will have to stay richly dressed and adorned throughout the waiting period!

Although Periyavāccān̲'s given name of Kṛṣṇapātar seems to indicate that it was Viṣṇu's form as Kṛṣṇa that was his special family deity, he seems to have had great empathy for Rāma.

Throughout his commentary on the *Nācciyār Tirumoḻi* he makes frequent references to the *Rāmāyaṇa.* To him, it seems obvious that Āṇṭāḷ's expression of love and longing should be compared to the emotion of Sītā, abducted and isolated in the Aśoka garden in Laṅkā. Though both Āṇṭāḷ and Sītā suffer the intense pangs of separation from the beloved, the vast difference in circumstances gives a different coloring to the two incidents. Young Āṇṭāḷ, on the threshold of womanhood, was waiting for her beloved to appear, longing for fulfillment; Sītā, on the other hand, was secure in the possession of the love of her beloved spouse. To Periyavāccāṉ Piḷḷai, however, Āṇṭāḷ was always Bhūdevī; he saw her as the accepted beloved of Viṣṇu, incarnated on earth as a devotee and temporarily separated from him. To those who view Āṇṭāḷ as a mystic and a saintly woman but nevertheless a human being who chose the way of love, viewing herself as the betrothed of god and yearning for fulfillment, the comparison with Sītā seems not totally appropriate. Again Periyavāccāṉ's comparison is based on the inner condition of *viraha tapa,* and the fact that both Sītā and Āṇṭāḷ were accepted incarnations of Bhūdevī. Later writers such as Piṉpaḻakiya Jīyar who wrote the Vaiṣṇava hagiography, *Kuruparamparāpirapāvam 6000*, appear to build on this comparison initiated by Periyavāccāṉ Piḷḷai.

One must concede, however, that Āṇṭāḷ and Sītā find common ground when they express their inability to live without the beloved. "How can I live/without the lord of Vēṅkaṭa" Āṇṭāḷ laments in the opening verse of her *Nācciyār Tirumoḻi.* She feels that only a token from her lord—be it his bangle, his yellow silk, his garland of sacred basil, the nectar of his mouth—will soothe her pain and keep her alive (hymn 13). Sītā, guarded by demonesses on the island of Laṅkā, contemplated suicide (*Sundarakāndam*, Ch. 26, vv. 44–51), her faith reviving only on receiving Rāma's ring from monkey–king Hanumān. The Vaiṣṇava approach totally accepted the Rāma–Sītā story and its traditional conjugal relationship. It almost appears as if Periyavāccāṉ Piḷḷai brought in constant comparisons with Sītā in order to justify Āṇṭāḷ's longing for her dark lord. Else the mystical approach to the beloved, expressed in terms of physical passion by a young woman, however saintly, might have been misunderstood by the general reader or by the pious. The Rāma avatar was the human ideal to follow; Kṛṣṇa's freedom was the freedom of a god and would not abide human questioning. A traditional exponent of the Puranic stories exhorted his listeners thus: "Admire the exploits of Kṛṣṇa, sing his praises; but follow in the footsteps of Rāma." In the context of Āṇṭāḷ and Sītā, a similar comparison would seem to reflect Periyavāccāṉ Piḷḷai's sentiments.

Glossary

Flora and Fauna

akil	a fragrant wood; eagle–wood.
āmpal	water–lily.
campakam	fragrant large yellow flower of the magnolia family. (*Michelia champaca*)
erukku	a milky shrub. (*Callotropis gigantea*)
indragopa	scarlet ladybug that appears after the rains, the cochineal.
katampa	waterside Indian oak. (*Nanclea kadamba*)
kalā	thorny shrub bearing an edible berry; whortle–berry. (*Vaccinium nilgherrense*)
kaṟanīr	red water–lily. (*Nymphaea rubra*)
karuviḷai	a wild creeper with dark blue flowers. (*Clitoria ternatea*)
kāyā	dwarfish tree with purple flowers and bilberries. (*Memecylon malabaricum*)
kayal	carp fish.
kuvaḷai	water lily. (*Pontederia*)
kārkōṭal	mangrove tree.
kōnku	buttercup tree with showy white or scarlet

	flowers; also known as the silk–cotton tree (*Bombax gossypinum*)
konrai	cassia or laburnum tree, with yellow clusters of flowers.
kōvai	climbing vine with red fruit and small flowers. (*Bryonia grandis*)
kurukatti	prickly wild poppy. (*Argemore mexicana*)
kurunti	a species of wild lime.
kuyil	koelbird; Indian cuckoo.
maruta	tropical tree with leaves clustered at ends of branches. (*Terminalia alata*)
mātavī	large creeper. (*Gaertnera macemosa*)
matta	datura tree; its flowers have narcotic properties. (*Datura fastuosa*)
mullai	jasmine.
murakka	Indian coral tree with showy crimson flowers, popularly known as "Flame of the Forest." (*Erythrina Indica*)
ñālal	wild thorny tree; the tigerclaw tree.
paṭā	mangrove tree.
pankaya	lotus. (Sanskrit: *pankaja*)
punnai	Alexandrian laurel tree.
pūvai	bilberry. (*kāyā*)
ceruntī	golden–blossomed wild pear tree. (*Ochna sqarrhosa*)

tulasī — sacred basil of god Vishnu.

vaḷai — cutlass fish. (*Trichiurus lepturus*)

vēmpu — margosa tree with bitter inedible fruit. (*Azadirachta Indica*)

Select Bibliography

Āṇṭāḷ Aruḷiceyta Nācciyār Tirumoḻi: *Itarku Periyavāccāṉ Piḷḷai Aruḷiceyta Vyākhyānamum Pūrvarkal Cērtavarum Pāṭamum Patavuraiyum.* (Tamil) Madras, 1923.

Arunachalam M. 1969. *Tamiḻ Ilakkiya Varalāru. Tamiḻ Pulavar Varalāru.* Multiple volumes. Tirucirrambalam: Gandhi Vidyalaya.

Cutler, Norman. 1979. *Consider Our Vow: An English Translation of Tiruppāvai and Tiruvempāvai.* Madurai: Muthu Patippakam.

———. 1987. *Songs of Experience: The Poetics of Tamil Devotion.* Bloomington: Indiana University Press.

———. Forthcoming. "The Making of the Pāvai Poems," in Holly Baker Reynolds, ed. *Brides of God, Brides of Men. Saint, Song, and Gender in a Tamil Devotional Tradition.*

Dehejia, Vidya. 1988. *Slaves of the Lord: The Path of the Tamil Saints.* Delhi: Munshiram Manoharlal.

Filliozat, Jean. 1972. *Un texte tamoul de dévotion vishnouite. Le Tiruppāvai d'Āṇṭāḷ.* Pondicherry: Institut Français d'Indologie.

Hardy, Friedhelm. 1983. *Viraha Bhakti.* Delhi: Oxford University Press.

Hart, George L. 1975. *The Poems of Ancient Tamil.* Berkeley: University of California Press.

Hooper, J.S.M. 1929. *Hymns of the Āḻvārs.* Calcutta: Association Press.

Hudson, Dennis. 1980. "Bathing in Krishna: A Study in Vaishnava Hindu Theology," *Harvard Theological Review*, vol. 73:539–566.

______. 1982. "Pinnai, Krishna's Cowherd Wife," in John Stratton Hawley and Donna Marie Wulff, eds. *The Divine Consort: Radha and the Goddesses of India*. Berkeley: Berkeley Religious Studies Series. 238–261.

______. Forthcoming. "Āṇṭāḷ's Enjoyment of God" in Holly Baker Reynolds ed. *Brides of God, Brides of Men: Saint, Song, and Gender in a Tamil Devotional Tradition.*

Iyengar, Ramaswamy D. 1946. *Thiruppāvai (with an English rendering)*. Madras: Teacher's Publishing House.

Kasthuri, R. 1971. *Pāvai Pāṭalkal*. Trivandrum: Kerala Co–op Stores Press.

Krishnaswami Aiyangar. ed. 1955. *Nācciyār Tirumoḻi Vyākhyāna*. (Tamil), Tiruchirapalli: Puttur Akraharam.

______. ed. 1968. *Ārāyirappaṭi Kuruparamparāpirapāvam*. Tiruchirapalli: Puttar Akraharam.

______. ed. 1984. *Tiruppāvai*. Tiruchirapalli: Puttur Akraharam.

Meenakshisundaram, T. P. 1968. "Tiruppāvai, Tiruvempāvai in Southeast Asia," *Proceedings of the First International Conference Seminar of Tamil Studies*. Kuala Lumpur: International Association of Tamil Research:11–20.

O'Flaherty, Wendy Doniger. 1975. *Hindu Myths*. New York: Penguin.

Ramanujan, A. K. 1967. *The Interior Landscape, Love Poems from a Classical Tamil Anthology*. Bloomington: Indiana University Press.

______. 1973. *Speaking of Śiva*. Baltimore: Penguin.

______. 1981. *Hymns for the Drowning. Poems for Viṣṇu by Nammāḻvār*. Princeton: Princeton University Press.

______. 1982. "On Women Saints," in John S. Hawley and D. M. Wulff, eds. *The Divine Consort: Rādhā and the Goddesses of India*. Berkeley: Berkeley Religious Studies Series: 238–261.

______. 1985. *Poems of Love and War: From the Eight Anthologies and the Ten Long Poems of Classical Tamil*. New York: Columbia University Press.

Ramanujan A.K. and Norman Cutler. 1981. "From Classicism to Bhakti," in Bardwell L. Smith, ed. *Essays on Gupta Culture*. Delhi: Motilal Banarsidass: 177–194.

Reynolds, Holly Baker. ed. Forthcoming. With contributions by Norman Cutler, Dennis Hudson, Holly Baker Reynolds, Glenn Yocum, and Katherine Young. *Brides of God, Brides of Men: Saint, Song, and Gender in a Tamil Devotional Tradition.*

Śrī Āṇḍāḷ. Her Contributions to Literature, Philosophy, Religion and Art. 1985. A compilation of lectures during All India Seminar on Āṇḍāḷ: August 13–15, 1983. Madras: Sri Ramanuja Vedanta Center.

Subramaniam, T. N. ed. 1953–57. *South Indian Temple Inscriptions*. Vol. 1–3, Madras: Govt. Oriental Manuscripts Library.

Sundaram, P.S. 1987. *The Poems of Āndāl (Tiruppavai and Nacciyar Tirumozhi)*. Bombay: Ananthacharya Indological Research Institute.

Venkatachari, K. K. A. 1978. *The Maṇiprāvaḷa Literature of the Śrīvaiṣṇava Ācāryas: 12th to 15th Century A.D.* Bombay: Ananthacarya Indological Research Institute.

Venkatachari, K.K.A. and T. A. Sampath Kumaracharya. eds. 1978. *Divyasūri Caritam by Garuḍa Vāhana Paṇḍita with*

Hindi rendering by Paṇḍita Mādhavāchārya. Bombay: Ananthacharya Research Institute.

Yocum, Glenn. Forthcoming. "Māṇikkavācakar and the "Pāvai Festival" at Avadayarkoil" in Holly Baker Reynolds, ed. *Brides of God, Brides of Men. Saint, Song, and Gender in a Tamil Devotional Tradition.*

Younger, Paul. 1982. "Singing the Tamil Hymnbook in the Tradition of Rāmānuja: The *Adhyāyanotsava* Festival in Śrīraṅkam." *History of Religions*, vol. 21 no. 3: 272–293.

Index